HIS
PRESENCE
IN THE
MIDST
OF
YOU

HIS
PRESENCE
IN THE
MIDST OF YOU

by Charles Elliott Newbold, Jr.

Ingathering Press
306 Cumberland Cove Rd.
Monterey, TN 38574
931-839-8078

Ingathering Press
4809 Honey Grove Drive
Antioch, Tennessee 37013

Published by Ingathering Press
4809 Honey Grove Drive
Antioch, Tennessee 37013
(615) 333-6958
Fax (615) 834-6194

Unless otherwise noted, scripture quotations are taken from the King James Version of the Bible with certain words changed to their modern equivalent; for example, "thee" and "thou" have been changed to "you," and "saith" has been changed to "says." A few words and punctuation marks have been modernized.

Scripture quotations noted NAS are from the New American Standard Bible. Copyright © 1960, 1962, 1963, 1968, 1971, 1972, 1973, 1975, 1977 by The Lockman Foundation.

Scripture quotations noted NKJV are from The Holy Bible, New King James Version. Thomas Nelson Publishers. Copyright © 1983 by Thomas Nelson, Inc.

The literal and more accurate translation for the Greek word *ekklesia* which is "called-out-ones" or "assembly" has been used rather than the traditional translation, "church."

Library of Congress Catalog Card Number: 98-92767

ISBN 0-9647766-2-6

Printed in the United States of America

TABLE OF CONTENTS

preface

Written in first person from God's perspective, the messages in this book should intensify your awareness of the constant presence of Christ in your life, enhance your understanding of what it means to be the body of Christ in fellowship with others, stir up the ministry gifts upon you, and call you forth unto a perfect man, unto the measure of the stature of the fullness of Christ (*Eph. 4:13*).

God is calling forth a people in this hour who will sanctify themselves as a kingdom of priests to carry the ark of His presence into the world around them, in order to fulfill the great commission to "go" with the promise that "lo, I am with you always even unto the completion of the age" (*Matt. 28:20*).

May these prophecies bring you into the joyful presence of our Lord Jesus Christ.

THE PRESENCE OF THE LORD

o n e

I, the Lord your God, am coming...I am coming once again to My temple...I am coming to fill My temple with My glory. My presence is My glory.

You are the temple of My Holy Spirit *(1 Cor. 6:19)*, My household *(Eph. 2:19)*, a people called by My name *(Deut. 28:10; Acts 15:17)*. I am coming to you. I am coming to fill you with My glory, My presence.

I want more than anything to fill you with My presence. I am sanctifying [setting apart, separating] a people unto Myself, preparing them for My coming so that when I come, I will have a house, pure and undefiled, in which to dwell. I want to dwell among My people and within My people.

I am turning up My refiner's fire in this hour that I might separate a people as pure gold and silver from the dross of sin and flesh. Are you willing to be in that number? Do you long, even pine, for My glory to come to My people?

If you do, expect great and glorious things to begin happening to you, for I am coming. I am coming soon. I am coming in all My glory. I am coming on My great white horse, riding triumphantly into the city of Zion, My holy hill, My holy people. There I will dismount and seat Myself upon the great throne of My judgment. There I will separate the sheep from the goats.

There I will call forth My people.

I will give them a crown of glory. I will fill them forever. They will be for Me, My people. I will possess them and they will possess Me. I will be in them and they shall be in Me. We shall be one in spirit.

I will fill them with My glory, My presence. They will see Me as I am, and when they see Me as I am, they will become as I am (*1 John 3:2*).

I am releasing upon the face of the earth a people who will bear My image as a temple filled with My glory. They will be My presence in the earth, in all the world. I in them. They in Me. Do you want to be in that number? Are you personally willing to deny yourself of all self-centeredness, to take up your cross daily and follow Me?

I am coming to My people—a people called by My name. By what name are you called? Do you take pride in being a Baptist, Presbyterian, Methodist, Lutheran, Episcopalian, Roman Catholic, Orthodox, Pentecostal, Charismatic? These are the names you have given to yourselves. Are these places in your heart where everyone of you says, I am of Paul, I am of Apollos, I am of Cephas, and I am of Christ (*1 Cor. 1:12*)? These names represent the icons of self-worship around which you gather and to which you pay homage. These are your idols. These are the extensions of yourselves.

I am coming for a sanctified bride, one who has cleansed herself of all of her idolatries, one who has a heart and eyes only for Me, her beloved, Jesus. She has renounced her ties with sin, the world, the deeds of the flesh, and any hold Satan has upon her. She is free from those things.

I am coming for My body—a people who have been crucified, resurrected, ascended, and glorified in Me. I am coming for a people who have declared that I, Jesus, am their only head. They are an obedient people. They listen to and obey My Holy Spirit, because My Holy Spirit listens to Me and obeys Me, the head, just as I listen to and obey the absolute, sovereign will of My Father (*John 5:19, 30; 14:24; 16:13*).

We are Father, Son, and Holy Spirit, three-in-one, working in concert to rebuild for Us a people for our eternal habitation.

I long for My presence to fill My temple. Do you? Humble yourself in My sight. Allow Me to reveal the truth about your heart and life. Let Me show you your sins and your idols. Let Me empty you of self that I might pour you full of Me.

I am coming...I am coming soon...I am coming to fill My temple with My glory, My presence, and My power. Will you be ready?

p r a i s e

t w o

Always take the time to enter into My presence before doing anything. Seek My face before you seek My hand. Seek Me even before you seek My will. I desire more than anything to be in your midst, to be the Lord your God in the midst of you. I am a holy God, a righteous God, an exacting God.

I have chosen you to be My people, a royal priesthood, a holy nation, kings and priests unto Me, to worship Me, to be a people who are to the praise of My glory *(Eph. 1:12, 1 Pet. 2:9; Rev. 1:6)*. I have chosen you and set you aside from the world for this very purpose, that I might have a people of My own among whom I might show forth My glory.

Enter into My presence. Come before Me with singing, dancing, rejoicing, and the playing of instruments of praise. I delight in My holy ones. I rejoice in My righteous ones. You are My children, My family, My household, and I am the one Father of you all.

I desire that you worship Me in spirit and in truth *(John 4:23)*, and out of that worship will come an abiding relationship between us. I in you, you in Me. We are one in spirit. This is the kind of intimacy I desire to have with you.

I want this intimacy in worship and praise before I want to answer your prayers. When you seek My hand before you seek My face, I feel used of you. I cannot be manipulated. I want to meet your every need. I want to answer your questions. I want to heal your wounds and supply your needs. I cannot do that unless you have first been willing to make your sacrifices of praise unto Me.

Lift up your hearts to praise Me. Center your affections upon Me and not upon yourself and your needs. Think about what I want and need from you. Desire with all of your heart to fill My cup first, then I will come out from My holy throne room and meet your every need.

The highest service anyone can render unto Me is to worship Me in spirit and in truth. I created you for this reason. Men lose their way with Me when they think they have to achieve great works in My name.

I do not want your works. I want you. I want your love, your passion, your desire to be in My presence and for My presence to abide in you.

They who wait upon Me to be refreshed by Me will be My lights in the world. The world will see the sacrifices you make to worship and praise Me, and, through such sacrifices of self, I will draw others to Me.

Your praise of Me is the greatest testimony you can give in the world. It is your message. Your life of praise is your works. It is your sacrifice of self—laying aside your agendas, your plans, and your programs to allow Me to be all in all.

When you come into My presence to praise and worship Me, concentrate upon Me. Fix your eyes and your heart upon Me. Do not allow your thoughts to wander. Do not be distracted by the movement of life round about you. Do not praise Me to get Me to do what you want Me to do. Do not praise Me to make a show of yourself. Rather, enter into your closets and minister to Me in secret.

When you come into My presence, you come into My glory.

When you come into My glory, My glory fills your house. My presence is My glory and My glory is My presence, and the more you come into My presence and My glory, the more you will want to bask therein. You will cultivate a spiritual appetite for Me. You will want only Me. You will find the things of this earth detestable.

Anointing

three

*T*he anointing is My presence. I make Myself available to My people through the outpourings of My Holy Spirit. I and My Spirit are one. Where the Spirit of the Lord is, there I am, for I am the great I AM.

My Holy Spirit has been released upon the earth from the very beginning of creation. He is My agent for all that I do. He is the energy, the power that accomplishes My word. I am My word (*John 1:14*). I am Jesus, the author and perfecter of your faith (*Heb. 12:2*). I have sent My word forth from the beginning to make My heart known, that I might be loved, trusted and obeyed. Whenever I send My word, I send My Holy Spirit with it. He goes out before Me, as Me, to accomplish My will. My will is My word. It is My testimony.

My Holy Spirit is the anointing upon you to accomplish those things for which I have called you. Every anointing has a calling. Callings are specific tasks that I have assigned for each of you to do. Everyone has a different assignment; therefore, everyone has a different anointing.

Elijah had the anointing to preach repentance to captive Israel. The anointing to preach repentance was upon him so that wherever he went that anointing went with him. I went with him, for I was the anointing upon him. I was the Presence of his life and calling. Wherever he went, the anointing to preach repentance went with him. Conviction came about in the hearts of many whether he opened his mouth to speak or not. Those who did not repent as the result of the conviction in their hearts hardened their hearts.

John the Baptist likewise had this Elijah-spirit anointing upon him. He came preaching a baptism of repentance, crying out, "See, the Kingdom of God is at hand" (*Matt. 3:2-3*). He prepared the way for Me, but it was I who ushered in the Kingdom. I am My Kingdom.

Because John had this anointing for repentance, I asked the multitudes following him, "What did you go out into the wilderness to see? A reed shaken with the wind? A man clothed in soft raiment? A prophet? Yes. I say to you, and more than a prophet" (*Matt. 11:7-9*). Did they go out to John to see the novelty of a man dressed in sheepskin and eating locusts? No. They went out to him because they were drawn to the anointing upon him; that is, they were drawn to Me.

They were drawn specifically to My presence upon John that called them to turn from their wicked ways unto Me. His anointing was very specific. His anointing for repentance prepared the way for My coming.

Then I came. I came with My anointing. My anointing was without measure. I was the fullness of the Godhead bodily (*Col. 2:9*). I am all in all.

When I stood up in the synagogue in Nazareth that solemn day, I declared who I was in their midst. I said: "The Spirit of the Lord is upon Me, because He has anointed Me to preach the gospel to the poor; He has sent Me to heal the brokenhearted, to preach deliverance to the captives, and recovering of sight to the blind, to set at liberty those who are bruised, to preach the acceptable year of the Lord" (*Luke 4:18-19*).

John the Baptist knew who I was. He wanted the anointing upon Me to be confirmed to his disciples so that his followers would follow Me and not venerate him. For this reason John said by the influence of My Holy Spirit, "He must increase, but I must decrease" *(John 3:30)*.

Until I came, there was no one greater in the Kingdom of God than John; but when I came, he gave way to Me who was the greatest. He preached a baptism of repentance in preparation for the coming of the Kingdom. I preached repentance and ushered in the Kingdom, because My Kingdom and I are one.

So, I said to John's disciples, "Go and show John again those things which you hear and see: The blind receive their sight, the lame walk, the lepers are cleansed, the deaf hear, the dead are raised up, and the poor have the gospel preached to them" *(Matt. 11:4-5)*. These are those things I declared previously in the synagogue in Nazareth.

I and My presence are one. My presence is My anointing. Wherever I went, there I went in the fullness of My anointing. I am the Christ, the Son of the living God. There is none other besides Me.

This I declare again at the consummation of this age, for many will come saying, "I am the Christ," "Look, there is the Christ" *(Matt. 24:23)*. But I say to you, as I declared to John and his disciples then, there is none other. I come in My own name. I come in the name of the Lord.

g l o r y

f o u r

*M*y presence is My glory. My glory is My presence. When you sing songs to glorify Me out of the desires of your hearts, you invite Me to increase My presence in your midst. I want nothing more than to be the Presence in your midst.

I wanted this with Israel, but they were afraid of Me. They

feared Me because of their own sin. They knew that My presence would wipe away their sin, but they had rebellion in their hearts. They loved their idols more than Me. I wept over them. I weep over them. I am in eternity. I am eternity. A perpetual tear is shed over them. Know My heart, My people. Until you know My heart, you will not permit Me into your presence, and I want so much to be the Presence in your midst.

Moses went up on the mountain to meet Me. He wanted to see Me. He wanted to know Me. He wanted to be in My presence and have Me to be in his, to talk to Me and hear from Me. Oh, how I long for a people, even now, who will turn aside from the idolatrous loves of their lives to sup with Me and make room for Me at their table.

There will be such a people. They are those whose lamps are filled with oil, who will go the distance with Me, who will be invited in to sit with Me at My banquet table.

You are My temple *(1 Cor. 3:16)*, My holy house. I live inside of you, in your spirit-man. I have taken up My abode there, and I am bringing you out of Egypt to the promised land by way of the wilderness. I have work to do in your hearts and lives—a work I will complete before I come.

You are My spiritual tabernacle in whom I have chosen to establish My Kingdom. My Kingdom is within you *(Luke 17:21)*. I am bringing you from faith to faith *(Rom. 1:17)* and from glory to glory *(2 Cor. 3:18)*. If My glory is My presence, then I am bringing you into an increasing awareness of My presence: from presence to presence. Be assured of this, I am allowing My glory cloud to fall upon My people in this final hour. My glory shall return to My temple. My presence shall be fully manifested in My people. The glory of My latter house shall be greater than that of the former house *(Hag. 2:9)*.

You will see Me. I am revealing Myself to you before I come. As you see Me, you will become as I am *(1 John 3:2)*. As My presence increases in you and in your midst, My resurrection, transforming, and ascension power will be released upon you as well. I will manifest My sons and daughters inasmuch as I am conforming them into the image of My glorious son (*Rom. 8:29*).

Expect increased visitations from My Holy Spirit. Expect increased visitations of My glory, My presence. I am coming to you. You will sense My presence more and more, day by day.

I am driving off the fear, the darkness, the gloom, the sin. I am separating out for Myself a people who are called by My name; who love, trust, and obey Me; who are willing to bask in My presence; who are willing for Me to purge, purify, and cleanse them of all sins.

My Spirit has always been with you but is now increasing in intensity and in purpose. You shall see Me as I make manifest visitations among some of you. You will not only sense My Holy Spirit, but you will see Me manifested even as I was between the time of My resurrection and My ascension. I shall come to strengthen you, commission you, and send you out.

I will give to many of you the rod of My authority. You shall hold it up when you see Me holding it up. You shall cast it down when you see Me casting it down. If it turns into a snake, it will eat Pharaoh's snakes (*Exod. 7:10-12*).

My presence shall come mightily upon many of you as I set you where I will into My body, returning to the foundation of the apostles and prophets, where I Myself am the chief corner-stone (*Eph. 2:20*).

If anyone claims to be an apostle or prophet but does not manifest My presence, he is not of Me. The true ones show forth Me, for I am the spirit of the apostle and the prophet. "For the testimony of Jesus is the spirit of prophecy" (*Rev. 19:10*).

P O W E R

f i v e

$\mathcal{M}$y presence is My power. Wherever you see My power at work, you can know that I am in your midst. I and My power are one.

When Elijah stood on the mountain against the prophets of Baal, he was not alone. I was there with him. I was with him in word and in deed. He said what he heard Me saying, and I performed what I said I would do. I was the fire that came down out of heaven to consume his water baptized altars (*1 Kings 18*).

My power created the heavens and the earth. My power separated the waters from the land. My power created man and called him forth by My breath while I held him in My hand. My power divided the Red Sea for My people to cross over on dry land. My power led them through the wilderness, fed them My manna, and gave them My water. I nurtured them for forty years while they yet rebelled against Me. My power pulled down the walls of Jericho. My power defeated their enemies in war. My power led them into exile and brought them back in My timing.

My power was present when I was conceived in the womb of Mary as the only begotten Son of God, Jesus, the Christ. My power was present on the cross to wipe away the sins of the world. My power was present when I was raised from the dead. My power was present when I poured out My Holy Spirit at Pentecost.

My power was present to heal the sick, give sight to the blind, give strength to the lame, cleanse the leper, raise the dead.

My power is My presence, and My presence is My power. My power is My grace. My grace is My presence. Grace is a power. Grace is not a cover for all the ways you fail to do My will (*John 1:12*). It is the power I give you to do My will. It is not the pardon of sin but the power of a sinless life. Grace is My empowering presence that enables you to do what I have called you to do and be what I have called you to be.[1]

My grace is sufficient. When you are weak, I am strong. When you try to be strong in your own strength, I allow you this liberty. When you become weak in your own strength and surrender to My power, I move upon your need and meet it. When you step in, I step back. When you step back, I step in. You choose most of the time which way it shall be.

My presence is My grace and My grace is My presence. When I am present, I am free to be the power at work in your life. I sustain you. I empower you. I give you My grace; that is to say, I give you that measure of Me you need for a given problem or situation in your life.

If you need to be born again by My Spirit, My presence comes into your spirit and gives you that new life. With that new life comes the need to walk in righteousness, even as I am altogether righteous. You need the power of My lordship. You cannot endure the requirement of righteousness in your own strength. Therefore, I baptize you in My Holy Spirit and power. I enable you with grace and power to walk in righteousness and holiness. I am your ability to love Me, trust Me, and obey Me.

The only thing that hinders you from love, trust, and obedience is failure to apprehend My sustaining presence in your life. Please know that I am with you all the days of your life, for I am your Good Shepherd.

Have I not said, I will never leave you nor forsake you (*Deut. 31:6,8; Josh. 1:5; Heb. 13:5*)? Have I not said that what I have started is mine to complete (*Phil. 1:6*)? Have I not said that all things work together for good to those who love Me and are called according to My purpose (*Rom. 8:28*)? Have I not said that the steps of a good man are ordered by the Lord, that I delight in his way? Though he fall, he shall not be utterly cast down, for I uphold him with My hand (*Ps. 37:23-24*).

Understand this one thing: I am always with you and My constant presence is My abiding power—power to save and power to keep. I am the Lord God Omnipotent.

---

[1] Few things are original. God often uses input from other sources under the anointing to reveal His word. I heard this definition of grace from a teaching by James Ryle.

I AM

s i x

I am the answer to your prayers when those prayers are offered in My name and according to My will.

I am the Alpha and Omega: the beginning and the end. I am your righteousness and your salvation, your strength and your joy. I am your justification, your redemption, your sanctification, your deliverance, your healing, and your glorification. I am the shepherd and guardian of your soul, the author and perfecter of your faith, and the apostle and high priest of your calling. I am your physician, your provider, your protector, and your peace. I am your all in all. I am Jehovah Jesus.

I was the fire in the burning bush, the Presence on the mountain. I was the voice that called out to Moses and said, "Don't come here; take off your shoes from your feet, for the place whereon you stand is holy ground" *(Exod. 3:5)*. I was the voice that said to him, "I am the God of your fathers—the God of Abraham, the God of Isaac, and the God of Jacob" *(Exod. 3:6)*.

I was the Presence on the mountain that day and Moses was afraid to look at Me *(Exod. 3:6)*. I was the call that went out to him to commission him to go to Pharaoh and bring My people out of bondage in Egypt *(Exod. 3:10)*, for I had seen their oppression and heard their cry *(Exod. 3:7)*.

Moses, understanding that he alone was a mere man, broke before Me and answered Me, "Who am I that I should go to Pharaoh, and that I should bring the children of Israel out of Egypt?" *(Exod. 3:11)*.

I said to him, "I will surely be with you" *(Exod. 3:12)*. He had already seen what could happen to him when he tried to answer My call in his own strength, when he killed the Egyptian *(Exod. 2:11-12)*.

I called him out of exile and promised My presence, that I would go up with him, and I would deliver My people by the might of My right hand.

I gave him My name so he and all the people would know who was leading them out. I said to him, "I AM THAT I AM" (*Exod. 3:13-15*). Tell the people that I AM has sent you to them. I AM the Presence in your midst. Without Me you could do nothing.

To strengthen the promise of My presence upon him and in the midst of them, I gave him a rod (*Exod. 4:1-9*). I gave him the rod of God. The rod was representative of My presence. Where My presence is, there also is My power and My authority. With many other signs I proved My word, My power, My intentions, and My presence to them.

I AM THAT I AM. I AM Jehovah—Jesus. The Jews questioned Me, how I could say I was greater than Abraham who is dead; that is to say, that I came before him, yet I was not even 50 years of age. I said to them, "Before Abraham was, I AM"[2] (*John 8:58*).

I am the one who spoke with the Samaritan woman at the well (*John 4*), and she knew because of My presence that I AM the Messiah to come (*John 4:25*). I AM the bread of life (*John 6:35,48*), the living bread which came down from heaven (*John 8:23*). I AM the door of the sheep (*John 10: 7-8*). I AM the good shepherd (*John 10:1*). I AM the resurrection and the life (*John 11:25*). I AM the way, the truth, and the life (*John 14:6*). I AM the true vine (*John 15:1*).

I told the Jews then, as I tell you now, that I AM is the Presence in your midst. "If you do not believe that I AM, you will die in your sins" (*John 8:24*). I had been saying to them from the beginning, if only they had ears to hear, that I AM THAT I AM. I said to them, "But when you lift up the Son of Man, then you will know that I AM" (*John 8:28*).

So it happened, when Judas brought the soldiers to arrest Me, I asked, "Whom are you seeking?" I wanted them to know that it was the great I AM they were arresting.

---

[2] Each I AM reference from John's gospel quoted above are from two Greek words, *ego eimi*, which literally translates "I, I am." In each of these references, Jesus was declaring that He was I AM THAT I AM, Yahweh (Jehovah), whose name was revealed to Moses.

They answered Me saying, "Jesus of Nazareth."

I answered them, "I AM."

When I spoke that word of revelation, they drew back from Me and fell to the ground. I asked them again who they were seeking. Again, they said, "Jesus of Nazareth."

I answered them a second time (two is the number of witness). "I have told you that I AM" *(John 18:1-8).*

I am Yahweh in the midst of you. Just as I was the great I AM then, so am I the great I AM today. I change not. I am the same yesterday, today, and forevermore *(Heb. 13:8).*

f r u i t

s e v e n

*T*herefore, because I am the great I AM, the Presence in your midst, I am in you and you are in Me. We are one.

I am the vine and you are the branches. He who abides in Me and I in him brings forth much fruit. Without Me you can do nothing *(John 15:5).* With Me you can bear fruit a hundredfold. You bear fruit according to your planting. If you plant plentifully, you will bear plentifully. I say, "Except a grain of wheat falls into the ground and dies, it abides alone; but if it dies, it brings forth much fruit" *(John 12:24).*

Fruit is the result of the kind of life that is in the tree. If you are a branch on a fig tree, you will bear figs. If you are a branch on a grapevine, you will bear grapes. The branch taken from the fig tree cannot be grafted into the grapevine and be expected to bear grapes. The branch has to be of like nature with the vine.

When you come to Me in faith, I come to you in power. I fill your life with My life. You become as I am. We are one of like nature. I abide in you and you abide in Me. I do not become your nature. You become mine. I am the Presence within you.

The fruit we bear together is "love, joy, peace, patience, kindness, goodness, faithfulness, gentleness, self-control…" (*Gal. 5:22-23 NAS*).

More than this, you become My presence in the world. A transformation takes place. You have been crucified with Me. It is no longer you who live but Me who lives in you; and the life you now live in the flesh, you live by My faith. I am He who loved you and gave Himself for you (*Gal. 2:20*).

You have measures of Me as My ambassadors (*2 Cor. 5:20*). As ambassadors, you represent Me in all that you do, in all of the places you go, and in all things you say. Therefore, when you speak, let your speech be as the oracles of God; if you minister, let it be by the ability which I give (*1 Pet. 4:11*). Be careful where you take Me, for you can defile My sanctuary, My presence. You can grieve My Holy Spirit. Therefore, be careful what you watch, where you go, what you listen to, and what you say. In such things you live, and move, and have your being.

Hear My heart, My holy ones. I have chosen you. I desire to indwell you. I desire to walk with you, talk with you. I desire to be the one in whom you live, and move, and have your being. You cannot abide in the world and in Me at the same time. "Love not the world, neither the things in the world. If any man loves the world, the love of the Father is not in him" (*1 John 2:15*).

You do love Me because you abide in Me. I am the presence in your midst and the presence within you. If you truly love Me, you will obey Me. You will keep My commandments (*John 14:15*). You will surrender your whole heart, soul, mind and strength. If you love Me, you will love your neighbor as yourself (*Mark 12:30-31*). "All men will know that you are My disciples, if you have love one to another" (*John 13:35*).

This love for one another is the fruit of being in Me. I am love. How can you be in Me and not love your fellowman? Your love for Me as shown to one another is how other men will see Me, for "no man has seen God at any time. If we love one another, God dwells in us, and His love is perfected in us" (*1 John 4:12*).

Now hear this: "If you abide in Me, and My words abide in you, you shall ask what you will, and it shall be done unto you" *(John 15:7)*. Why? Because you are My presence in the world. By this I am glorified. My glory is My presence. The more you abide in Me, the more fruit you will produce. You are My fruit. The greater your fruit, the more I am glorified; that is, My presence is increased. The greater My presence, the greater the fruit *(John 15:7-8)*.

I prayed for you in the midnight hours before My sacrifice. What I pray is true. It comes to pass. I prayed for you who believe in My name, that you all may be one as the Father is in Me and I in Him—that you may also be one in us. By this the world will know that the Father has sent Me.

I prayed for the glory (My presence) that the Father gave Me be given to you. Abiding in My presence and having My presence abiding in you is the only basis for oneness among you. I prayed that you might be made perfect in that oneness.

Moreover, I prayed out of the deep desire of My heart that all of you whom the Father gave Me might be where I am, that you might experience My presence and see the glory the Father has given Me *(John 17)*.

Yes, I prayed for you then, and do so now, that you may have eyes to see and ears to hear of the glorious appearing of your Lord—I AM.

w e a k n e s s

eight

When you understand the power of My presence, you will never again want to depend upon the strength of your own flesh. My servant Paul understood this. He wrote to the

Corinthian believers that he had come to them in weakness, fear, and much trembling. He had determined not to know anything among them except Me and My crucifixion (1 Cor. 2:1-3).

His speech and his preaching were not with persuasive words of human wisdom, but in demonstration of My Spirit and of My power. He did not want their faith to be based on anything other than My power (1 Cor. 2:4-5).

Nevertheless, he spoke of the great mysteries which I had hidden before the ages. He spoke of them for their glory and for yours (1 Cor. 2:7); that is, to demonstrate My presence in their midst. He went to them in weakness but I was his strength. In his moment of need, I manifested My presence through the power of My Holy Spirit to reveal these mysteries to them.

I choose the weak things of the flesh to show forth the power and might of My Spirit. I want to show forth My glory. I want to manifest My presence. I want to make a show of My mighty works, not of men's, that I might be known of men.

Even though I had revealed great mysteries to My servant Paul through visions and revelations, even catching him up to the third heaven, I had to keep him weak in his own estimation of himself. Therefore, I allowed a messenger from Satan to buffet him, to keep him in reality, to remind him constantly that it was not him doing these mighty deeds, but Me—that it was not about him, but about Me. Therefore, I told him that My grace was sufficient for him. My power was made perfect in his weakness (2 Cor. 12:1-10).

Men become arrogant in what they think they know. They become puffed up by who they think they are. In so doing, they demonstrate their failure to understand who I am and what I am doing in their midst.

The flesh has no power and has to rely upon manipulation and control in order to get its way. Manipulation and control is the practice of witchcraft in the broad sense of that word. Therefore, when men begin to put confidence in their own flesh, they invite the ruling spirit of witchcraft into their midst. I take flight. I will not abide where manipulation, control, and heavy-handedness exist.

Men who seek control over others are insecure. They do not know Me. Therefore, they cannot trust Me. They think they have to trust in themselves. In so trusting in themselves, they become prideful in the works of their own hands that were birthed in the imaginations of their minds. They give birth to idols and name them after Me.

I am jealous for My people. I want to be the Presence in the midst of you. I do not want your self-inflated egos to be in the midst of you. I do not want your idols—those extensions of yourself—to be in the midst of you. Those idolatries of yours are harlotries to Me.

My presence is often not wanted in those very places you would expect to find Me. Therefore I am found standing outside the door knocking, begging for you to open up that I might come into where you are, to sup with you and you with Me, that our fellowship might be complete (*Rev. 3:20*).

I am a jealous God. I am jealous to be the Presence in the midst of you. Drive out your prideful icons of self-worship, humble yourself in My sight, fall in love with Me, surrender all—yes even this: deny yourself of your self-centeredness, take up your cross of self-denial, bear it, come, and follow Me (*Matt. 16;24*).

Walk with Me, talk with Me, love Me, praise Me, worship Me, trust Me. Get out of the way, step aside, and allow Me to be the Presence in the midst of you.

THE
BODY

nine

I write these things to you that you might become increasing-ly aware of My presence in you, on you, and among you. Many who are true believers, who have been born again by My Spirit from above, have had an awareness of My presence from time to time. Because the awareness of My presence is not constant-ly "felt," they presume that I come and go. There is little aware-ness that I am perpetually present.

Many others who know Me by name only, should know by these writings that there is far more of Me available to them than they have ever hoped for, far more than they could imag-ine. Oh, how I want to be the Presence in the midst of you!

I want fellowship. I want partnership. I want to share My life, My power, My joy, My peace with My people. I want to dance with you, talk intimately with you. I want to participate in all of who you are and have you to participate in all of who I am. This is the communion, the *koinonia*[3] I seek.

Your fellowship is with the Father and with Me, the Son, Jesus Christ *(1 John 1:3)*, and is in the Holy Spirit *(Phil 2:1; 2 Cor. 13:14)*. If you have true fellowship, partnership, participa-tion, sharing, communion, and communication with Me, you will have it one with another *(1 John 1:7)*.

You will see that you are one body in Me *(1 Cor. 12:12-31)*. If, indeed, you are many members of one body, then you are of the same essence. What you think, say, or do to one member of My body, you think, say, or do it to yourself. Moreover, you do it to Me. I and My body are one.

---

[3] *Koinonia* is the Greek word that has been translated communion, fellowship, participation, sharing, and communication.

When Saul was persecuting My assembly of called-out-ones, he was persecuting Me *(Acts 9:1-9)*. Remember I taught that inasmuch as you do it unto the least of others, you do it unto Me...Inasmuch as you fail to do it unto the least of others, you fail to do it unto Me *(Matt. 25:40,45)*. I cannot be separated from My body. My body cannot be separated from Me or from one another. This is a mystical union we have one with another *(Eph. 5:32)*.

My body is sick, diseased, distressed, sin-ridden, and many die because they do not rightly discern My body. They do not rightly discern one another as equally important members of My body *(1 Cor. 11:27-32)*. Therefore, My body is handicapped by division, criticism, judgmentalism, complaining, gossiping, and rivalry among you. You grieve My Holy Spirit when you backbite and bicker with one another.

Failure to receive a member of My body is the failure to receive Me. You cannot have Me in part. All of you must eat all of Me; that is to say, you must receive all of those who are Mine. This is why I required of Israel, as they were preparing their exodus from Egypt, to eat all of the flesh of the Passover lamb. What was not eaten by morning was to be burned by fire *(Ex. 12:8-9)*.

That Passover lamb foreshadowed Me, the Lamb of God *(John 1:29,36; 1 Pet. 1:19; Rev. 5:6)*. It was eaten in a family setting. They were to eat all of it and not allow any part of it to be unconsumed or defiled. So it is with My body today. "Take, eat, this is My body given for you" *(Matt. 26:26)*.

Except you eat My flesh and drink My blood, you have no life in you. "Whoever eats My flesh and drinks My blood has eternal life, and I will raise him up at the last day. My flesh is meat indeed, and My blood is drink indeed. He who eats My flesh and drinks My blood dwells in Me, and I in him. As the living Father has sent Me, and I live by the Father, so he who eats Me, even he shall live by Me" *(John 6:53-57)*.

Inasmuch as I gave My body for you, you all, as My body, are to give yourselves one to another. You each exist for the strengthening and well-being of the other.

When My body flows in oneness this way, My life blood is free to flow through its veins. I send life to all parts of the body for "the life is in the blood" *(Lev. 17:11).*

You are My body and individual members thereof. This is more than a metaphor. This is a Kingdom reality. Walk in the knowledge and power of it.

g a r *d* *e* n

t e n

C. Austin Miles knew very well My desire to walk in *koinonia* with you. Flowing out of his own life's experience, under the inspiration of My Holy Spirit, he set these words to music. These words express how I want to be in relationship with you.

"I come to the garden alone,
While the dew is still on the roses;
And the voice I hear,
Falling on my ear;
The Son of God discloses.

He speaks, and the sound of His voice
Is so sweet the birds hush their singing,
And the melody that he gave to me,
Within my heart is ringing.

And He walks with me, and He talks with me,
And He tells me I am His own,
And the joy we share as we tarry there,
None other has ever known."[4]

I not only wait within the garden of My heart to walk and talk with you, I am the garden. I am the still of the morning, the hush of the bird's song, the fragrance of the rose, the glistening of the fallen dew. My voice can be heard there. My will can be known there. This garden is a quiet place in Me.

My presence is made manifest in the stillness of My garden. Go there. Find Me there. This garden is likewise a quiet place in you. I in you, you in Me, returning, as it were, to that place of sweet fellowship even as I had with Adam in the garden of Eden.

The fall of man brought on the clutter and clamor of life— the busy schedules, the noisy freeways, the frenzy of time. These are little foxes that eat away at the vine and keep us from having that intimate time one with another.

Come away, My bride. Hide. Hide with Me in the garden. Steal away from your own self-driven lifestyle. Seek My face. Take pleasure in Me and not your flesh. Cultivate a hunger for more of Me that I might have all of what I paid for.

Here in My garden, the garden of who I am, you may eat of every tree. I am the tree of life. There is no longer a tree of the knowledge of good and evil in Me. That tree is rooted and grounded in the world. It is the tree from which worldly people eat. Yes, even more so. They are the branches of that tree and bear the fruit thereof.

You have been transformed into a different tree. You not only eat of the tree of life, but you are the branches of that tree and bear the fruit thereof. Yes, there is a sweet-smelling, quiet-place garden in Me. Come and see how pleasant it is to dwell there with Me.

The LORD your God in the midst of you is mighty; I will save, I will rejoice over you with joy; I will rest in My love, I will joy over you with singing (Zeph. 3:17).

PRESENCE
conscious

e l e v e n

I am the Lord your God in the midst of you. Do not forget that I am in your midst. I am with you when you rise up and lie down, when you go out and come in. I am always with you.

Make a conscious effort to remind yourself that I am with you, in you, and among you. Increase your awareness of Me in your presence. Failure to think of Me as always being with you gives you permission to walk in a way that is not pleasing to Me. You do things, say things, think things you would never do, say, or think if I were with you in flesh and blood. Yet, it is no different with Me. I am just as with you in spirit as I would be in the flesh.

When you have a Presence-consciousness, you will experience the anointing that goes with My presence. Where My anointing is, there is My power. More of My power is released through your awareness of Me.

As you train yourself to be Presence-conscious, you will learn to hear My still, small voice more audibly. You will gain confidence in our relationship. You will come to know Me better, to know My will and My ways. You will desire to know Me better day by day and desire to walk in faithfulness and obedience.

Thereby you will become more of who I am and begin to do as I say do, say what I say to say, and be who I have made you to be. You will experience My power working in your midst. I will go before you and drive out the enemy. I will be your rear guard.

As you become more Presence-conscious, you will be less likely to sin and take Me to places I do not wish to go. You will be less likely to grieve My precious Holy Spirit.

You will find a struggle, a war waging inside of you as you become more Presence-conscious. Your mind will want to take you places your spirit does not want to go. In your attempts to resist going there in your mind, you will find just how compelling your fleshly mind is. As you become more Presence-conscious, you will have more of My life and power, My grace, to resist this enemy of your mind.

The old man of flesh, likewise in agreement with your fleshly mind, will impulsively drive you to indulgences that are harmful to you and to others. It knows nothing other than to violate God, yourself, and others. It is ego-invested. It does only what it wants for self. Here again, as you become more Presence-conscious, you will have My life and My power to win the war against your flesh.

Think of Me as actually being there at all times and in all places, for indeed I am. While this may be unsettling to you when you are in the throes of temptation, it is of comfort to you to know that even I suffered temptation in the flesh (*Heb. 2:18*). Yet I overcame. I am the Presence in your midst to overcome your temptation for you. There is no condemnation in temptation.

Remind yourself constantly until it becomes automatic for you that I am with you always even to the completion of the age (*Matt. 28:19-20*). Have I not promised you that I will never leave you nor forsake you (*Deut. 31:6*)? "When you pass through the waters, I will be with you; and through the rivers, they shall not overflow you. When you walk through the fire, you shall not be burned; neither shall the flame kindle upon you" (*Isa. 43:2*).

Therefore, submit yourself to Me and resist the devil. Resist the devil of your fleshly mind. Resist the devil of your old man of flesh and sin. Resist the devil altogether, and he will flee from you. Draw near to Me and I will draw near to you (*Jas. 4:7-8*).

When you feel weak, impulsive, out of control in anything pertaining to ungodliness, reach out to Me. Touch Me. Be willing to be weak in that matter so that I might be your strength.

self-denial

t w e l v e

W hat does it mean to deny self?

You live in an old, fallen-man body of flesh that is self-centered, self-driven, and self-invested. Self is the center of your universe. Self knows only one thing: to get more for self so there will be more of self. Self has little or no regard for the needs of other selves and has little or no desire to meet the needs of other selves. It has no capacity within itself to deny itself of anything. It aggressively seeks to satisfy its every lust and impulse. It is depraved. It is on a fast track to self-destruction.

This fallen condition occurred at the beginning of time when I set Adam and his wife, Eve, in the garden of fellowship with Me. I told them to eat of all of the trees in the garden, but I told them not to eat of the tree of knowledge of good and evil. They could have eaten of Me, the Tree of Life, received My life, and been satisfied for all eternity.

Rather, being beguiled by the devil, they chose to eat of the forbidden fruit. They believed Satan's lie that they would become as I am, knowing good and evil. They came to know good and evil, but received the penalty of death rather than My life. They became flesh man.

They were no longer sons of God but became sons of Satan. You are the sons and daughters of the one you obey. They chose to come under Satan's lordship in that day. They became something other than what they had been made to be.

They went out from the garden of fellowship with Me and had children after their own kind. Those children had children after their own kind. From generation to generation so it was, and is, that all men and women are born into this world under the domain of Satan with the genetic code common to Adam after his fall.

Now, this old man of flesh is full of envy, lust, greed, hatred, idolatry, anger, drunkenness, fear, and murder. It is capable of all things vile and abusive. It has no power to be otherwise. It cannot change its nature. If the man of flesh is not transformed by My Spirit into My nature, it is subject to judgment and death. It cannot deny itself of anything.

Therefore, you must be born again. You must come to believe that I am God, that I am Jesus, the Christ, the Son of the living God. When I see you putting your faith and trust in Me with a willingness to obey Me, I consider you righteous. I, then, send forth My Spirit to come into your spirit to quicken you to new life in Me. You become a new creature in Me *(2 Cor. 5:17)*. You are now sons of God, the children of God. I have become your Lord and Master instead of Satan being so. I am your Father, your heavenly Father.

You now have My mind and My Spirit within you. I become the power within you to overcome the compulsions and impulses of your flesh. Nevertheless, your flesh still cries out to have its way, but you put it to death by denying it. You deny your flesh by your acts of obedience to Me.

For every act in the flesh, there is an action to counteract it in the spirit, but how are you to know what that counteraction is unless you seek Me? How are you to seek Me, if you do not have a sense of My presence in your life?

Therefore, you need more power; that is, more of Me. You need a greater intensity of My presence in your midst. I offer the fullness of My Holy Spirit to come upon you that you might have the power of My lordship in your life. I baptize you in My precious Holy Spirit. I immerse you, soak you, saturate you in My Spirit. Who among you would not want Me to give you this greater measure of Me?

I am the power in your life that enables you to deny yourself of self. You cannot do this in your own strength.

To deny self is to give up what you want for yourself that I might have what I want for you. Nevertheless, this old man of flesh is insidious, deceptive, and easily deceived. It often thinks that serving self is serving Me, but that can never be.

To obey is better than sacrifice *(1 Sam. 15:22)*. Obedience is the sacrifice. Obedience is the cross. So when you deny self, you are taking up a cross, the cross of self-denial. This is the only way anyone can follow Me. Whenever you discover My will in a matter, you will discover that something usually has to die in you. It has to be sacrificed.

flesh

t h i r t e e n

*F*lesh is the enemy to the free flow of My Spirit. It is self-centered, self-serving, prideful, arrogant, boastful, full of envy and jealousy, covetous, controlling, and manipulative. "Now the works of the flesh are evident, which are: adultery, fornication, uncleanness, licentiousness, idolatry, sorcery, hatred, contentions, jealousies, outbursts of wrath, selfish ambitions, dissensions, heresies, envy, murders, drunkenness, revelries, and the like" *(Gal. 5:19-20 NKJV)*.

Because the flesh is self-seeking, controlling, and manipulative, it is under the influence of the spirit of witchcraft. In a broad definition, witchcraft is anything one does to influence others to do things against their will. Witchcraft is a ruling spirit.

There are two main ruling spiritual spirits in the world: My Holy Spirit and the satanic influence of witchcraft. Witchcraft is the counterfeit to My Holy Spirit. These two influences are in opposition to each other.

My Holy Spirit is associated with submission to My divine will as revealed in My word. Witchcraft is associated with rebellion against My word *(1 Sam. 15:23)*. You are either ruled by My Holy Spirit or by the spirit of witchcraft. You are either obedient or rebellious to My Holy Spirit. If you are obedient to My Holy Spirit, then you are ruled by My Holy Spirit. If you are rebellious to My Holy Spirit, then you are ruled by the satanic influence of witchcraft.

My Holy Spirit is the only power that can change your nature. Those who have put their trust in Me and are born from above by My Holy Spirit have been transformed into a new creation (2 Cor. 5:17). Satan has no power to transform your nature. He can only influence your decisions and behaviors through fear, enticements, and unbelief. He has to resort to control and manipulation—witchcraft.

This spiritual influence of witchcraft is universal and is part of a hierarchy of principalities, powers, rulers of the darkness of this world, and spiritual wickedness in high places (Eph. 6:12). These all operate under the authority of Satan.

Therefore, whenever flesh is in operation, witchcraft is released to practice control and manipulation. When you see this happening, you will see how My Holy Spirit is hindered. Witchcraft binds; I release. Witchcraft wants to be in the spotlight; My Holy Spirit calls for humility. Witchcraft wants submission to her; true submission is unto Me. Witchcraft is deceitful; My Holy Spirit is the spirit of truth. Witchcraft casts a cloud of darkness and deception; My Holy Spirit is light and truth. These are just some of the ways witchcraft, operating under the authority of the flesh, can hinder the flow of My Spirit in the midst of you.

Moreover, witchcraft is a seductive spirit, further hindering My presence in the midst of you. The seductive aspect of witchcraft is the Jezebel spirit. The Jezebel spirit is anything for self. It is the harlotry of self. All of which is the work of the flesh.

Remember how that woman Jezebel seduced My bondservants to eat things sacrificed to idols (Rev. 2:20)? She seduced them to worship other gods. All idolatry is spiritual harlotry to Me. Idolatry is an extension of self, therefore it is self-worship. I am jealous of all the things you love more than Me.

You are being seduced anytime one draws your affection and

attention away from Me. They want something for themselves. They use flattery and manipulations of every kind to draw you into their web. Once there, you become a victim of their needs. They devour you and suck the life out of you in order to fatten their own egos.

Such are the ways of the Nicolaitans in the churches. Nicolaitan means "conqueror of the people."[5] They are those who have separated and elevated themselves as clergy over the rest of those who profess to be My followers. They are those in ministry who rule according to the flesh and not according to My Spirit. They are ambitious to advance themselves in power, position, and riches. They oppress and use My people for their own advantage. They do not exist to serve the people, but to bind people into serving them. They exercise tyranny over My people in spirit, soul, and body. This is an abomination to Me.

By demanding false allegiance to themselves—teaching a false doctrine of submission to their authority—these Nicolaitans have deceived My bond-servants and caused them to eat foods (defiled sermons and doctrines) sacrificed to demons (the idolatry of self-worship).

The deeds and the teachings of the Nicolaitans are grossly deceptive because they do them in My name. People are led to believe that their sacrifices of service and contributions of money to these Nicolaitans are as unto Me. This is a lie and a deception. It runs completely contradictory to Me, My will, My heart, and My word.

Those who practice these things are controlling, manipulative, and possessive. They claim ownership over people. Anyone at anytime who dares to cross them are made to feel rebellious, shameful, and defiled. They are abusive. They violate Me and the precious liberty I have given My bond-servants, for where My Spirit is, there is liberty (2 Cor. 3:17).

My servant Paul was inspired of Me to write the Galatian followers to stand fast in the liberty wherewith I had made them free

---

[5] The Nicolaitans are mentioned in Revelation 2:6 in reference to the assembly of called-out-ones in Ephesus. Nicolaitan in Greek is the combination of two Greek words: *nike* which means "conquer, overcome, subdue" and *laos* which refers to a body of people. Combined it translates "conqueror of the people."

and not to be entangled again with the yoke of bondage (*Gal. 5:1*).

Whenever you find your focus is upon another man or woman, rather than upon Me, your Lord and Master, you are being persuaded away from Me. Jezebel is standing in the door, enticing you away from Me.

Be aware of her flirtatious ways. Know, also, that the compulsive-obsessive nature of your old man of flesh is in agreement with the practice of witchcraft and the Jezebel spirit. Witchcraft spoils the beauty of My presence in the midst of you.

Either My Holy Spirit or witchcraft can be the presence in the midst of you. It is your call. If you want My Holy Spirit to be in control of your life, "ask, and it shall be given to you; seek, and you shall find; knock, and it shall be opened to you. Every one who asks receives, and he who seeks finds, and to him who knocks it shall be opened. If a son shall ask bread of any of you who is a father, will he give him a stone? Or if he asks a fish, will he for a fish give him a serpent? Or if he shall ask an egg, will he offer him a scorpion? If you then, being evil, know how to give good gifts unto your children, how much more shall your heavenly Father give the Holy Spirit to them who ask Him?" (*Luke 11:9-13*).

Therefore, guard your hearts and minds. Put to death any temptation to shine in your strength. Be willing to stand in the lesser lights, to surrender all fleshly desires for ministry, and be willing for Me to be your sufficiency—for Me, the Lord your God, to be the Presence in your midst.

If you are in ministry and building anything other than a people who are to the praise of My glory, you are caught up in vainglory and building in vain. You are building something for self.

The fleshly mind is at enmity against Me (*Rom. 8:7*). It always has been, is now, and ever shall be. Put to death the temptations of your flesh and the imaginations of your mind. I did not give you My liberty as an occasion for your flesh, but that you might have the liberty and God-given ability to love one another (*Gal. 5:13*). If you bite and devour one another, take heed that you not be consumed by one another (*Gal. 5:15*).

You shall learn this difference: When you operate according to your flesh, you will devour one another. If, on the other hand, you fellowship in My Spirit, commune with Me, allow Me to be the Presence in the midst of you, you will not seek your own but will strive to have all things in common. To have all things in common does not mean you are to pool your resources, but that each of you have common access to Me. Therefore you participate, share, fellowship, and have partnership in one another's lives. You are all many members of My one body. I am the common denominator in your midst.

Therefore, walk in a Presence-consciousness. Regard one another as having this same Presence. Hear and respect one another, listen to one another, be still, wait, show patience, regard one another with greater esteem than you do yourselves (Phil. 2:3). Yet, know that you are beloved of Me. I am your beloved and you are Mine (Song of Sol. 6:3).

Your flesh tendencies will always hinder the flow of My Spirit. Take this very seriously, especially when you come together in My name to partake of My body and My blood, because the flesh is contrary to Me. The flesh lusts [sets its desire] against My Spirit, and My Spirit against the flesh (Gal 5:17).

When you are in the free flow of My Spirit, you will bear the fruit of My Spirit which is "love, joy, peace, long-suffering, kindness, goodness, faithfulness, gentleness, and self-control" (Gal. 5:22-23 NKJV).

"This I say then, walk in the Spirit, and you shall not fulfill the lust of the flesh" (Gal. 5:16).

ABIDE

f o u r t e e n

*N*otice in John's gospel, chapter 14, what I said to My chosen ones. In comforting them, I told them that in a little while the world would no longer see Me, but that they would see Me. They would see Me in a way not possible for the world to see Me. They would see Me in the realm of the spirit, the supernatural, because I would be giving them the same kind of life that I am.

When they received this life, they would know within themselves that I am in the Father, they would be in Me, and I would be in them. Their obedience to Me would be proof of their love for Me. I told them that whoever loved Me would be loved by the Father. Moreover, I would love them and reveal Myself to them.

Judas (not Iscariot) could not understand how I would reveal Myself to them but not to the world. Here is how it works. If anyone loves Me—not just My disciples then, but anyone—he will keep My commandments, and My Father will come to him. We, My Father and I, will come to him and make our home with him.

If I and My Father come and make our home in you, you will understand what I meant when I said that My Father's house has many dwellings. You are our dwelling place, our mansions. My Father and I make our home in you; yet, you have your dwelling place in us. Thus, our house is in you and your house is in us. This is not a funeral service scripture. It is a present day reality expressing how I am the Presence in your midst.

If you see Me, you see the Father. I am in the Father and the Father is in Me. Now if the Father and I are in you and you are in us, then the works that We do, you will do. You will be doing what We do because We are one with you.

Therefore, whatever you ask in My name—that is, whatever you ask in the context of obedient love—will be done for you because it will be We doing the asking and the answering.

Therefore, you are to understand that while We most certainly want to be the Presence in your midst, We also want to manifest Our works through you. We indwell you that We might have a body through which to work Our great and glorious works.

Therefore, you are the presence of the Lord in your own midst. You are not God, but you are the revealed presence of God in the world.

Thus My presence in your life is the foundation for all ministry. You can do nothing apart from Me. It is never you doing the works of God, but We doing Our works through you.

Everywhere you turn in scripture you will see how I wanted only one thing: to abide in and with My people. Any other view of Me is doctrinal and erroneous, to be rejected.

MINISTRIES & GIFTS

f i f t e e n

"*B*ehold, a virgin shall be with child and shall bring forth a son, and they shall call his name Emmanuel, which being interpreted is, God with us" (*Matt. 1:23*).

I am Emmanuel, God with you. See, that is even My name. I come in the fullness of the Godhead (*Col. 2:9*) as the Apostle and High Priest of your profession (*Heb. 3:1*), the Shepherd and Overseer of your souls (*1 Pet. 2:25*), the author and finisher of your faith (*Heb. 12:2*). I had the Spirit without measure (*John 3:34*).

Then I ascended on high after My resurrection and gave gifts to men. I gave some to be apostles, some prophets, some evangelists, some pastors and teachers (*Eph. 4:11*). From the day of Pentecost I gave gifts of the Spirit: different gifts but all from the same Spirit.

I gave to one the word of wisdom, to another the word of knowledge, to another faith, to another the gifts of healing, to another the working of miracles, to another prophecy, to another the discerning of spirits, to another different kinds of tongues, to another the interpretation of tongues...dividing to each one separately as I willed *(1 Cor. 12:8-11)*. Some are given the gift of exhortation, giving, ruling, or mercy *(Rom. 12:6-8)*. Some are given helps and some administration [governments] *(1 Cor 12: 26)*. Some are psalmists and some receive revelations *(1 Cor. 14:26)*.

These and many more ministry gifts of My Spirit are given to men and women for the edification of My body. When I ascended on high, having the fullness of these ministries and gifts without measure, I poured Myself back into the members of My body, each having a measure of some ministry or gift.

I chose to do this in order to make you dependent one upon the other, that you might be a community of believers in Me; so that when you come together as members of My body, everyone of you has the potential to bring forth a psalm (but especially the psalmists), or a teaching (especially the ones anointed for teaching), or a tongue, or a revelation, or an interpretation *(1 Cor. 14:26)*.

I have set you in My body as I will *(1 Cor. 12 18)*. It is not your prerogative to bounce around from church to church but to seek My face and My will that you might be fitly framed together and grown into a holy temple for Me *(Eph. 2:21)*. I am assembling you, especially now in this last hour before I come. I am tabernacling you into small family units that I might come to you in the fullness of My presence and glory.

Those who want to bask in My presence and My glory will hear My Spirit's voice and obey Him as He builds the house that I am building. Find your place in the body.

Then, do not forsake the assembling of yourselves together; that is, do not forsake the balanced coming together of these various ministries and gifts, that you might consider how to stir up love and good works among you, exhorting one another, and so much the more as you see the day of My coming approaching *(Heb. 11:23-25)*.

Each one of you, especially the equipping gift ministries of apostles, prophets, evangelists, pastors [elders] and teachers, are given to equip the saints for the work of service which is the work of building up My body. You are to keep on doing this until you all come to the unity of the faith and the knowledge of the Son of God, to a perfect man. This work of My Spirit within and through each of you continues to the end until you all measure up as one man to the stature of the fullness of Christ *(Eph. 4:11-13).*

Therefore I, who had the fullness of ministry and gifts, poured Myself out into each of you in measure, that you may drink of Me from one another's cup and be made full.

When you come together, you bring Me with you. I become the Presence in the midst of you. I then stir up the gifts among you that you might offer up unto Me the high praises that I and I alone am worthy to receive. I stir you up to worship Me in spirit and in truth, for I seek such people to worship Me *(John 4:23).* I inhabit the praises of My people, Israel *(Ps. 22:3).*

All of you who put your trust in Me and are born again by My Spirit are My Israel. You who worship Me in Spirit and rejoice in Christ Jesus and have no confidence in the flesh are My true circumcision *(Phil. 3:3),* for you are not a Jew outwardly in the flesh, but inwardly. It is a circumcision of the heart. It is a circumcision in the spirit and not in the letter of the law. It is a circumcision whose praise is from Me and not from men *(Rom. 2:28-29).* You who believe in Me are My faithful ones. I am the Presence in the midst of you.

Wherever I am, My gifts are in operation. I minister to My people. The gift I gave you is a portion of Me that I want to pour out into others. It, therefore, behooves each of you who want Me to place you in My body where I will, to be filled with My Holy Spirit, to be immersed in My Spirit that I might give you the ministries and gifts of My Spirit, that I might use you to pour Me out one to another as I conform you into My image.

It is imperative that you first be baptized fully into My Holy Spirit, to hunger and thirst for all of who I am. It is imperative that you learn to hear My voice, that you practice obedience in the context of My body, meeting in small family groups as I fit you one to another, as I set you in place as living stones one to another. You will not fit if you do not submit one to another.

I will manifest My presence in your midst through your willingness to obey Me in saying the words I give you to say, singing the songs I give you to sing, speaking the revelations I give you to share, reading the scriptures I give you to read, and praying the prayers I give you to pray. I will come to you. It will be Me, not you, being the gifts you are.

Through your obedience, then, I will release My power to save, baptize in My Spirit, deliver from evil, and heal My body. I long to be the Presence in the midst of you, and I have chosen to distribute Myself in part in each of you that you might bring your part of Me into your assemblies and enjoy the fullness of Me. In the presence of the Lord, there is fullness of joy, and at My right hand there are pleasures forevermore *(Ps. 16:11)*.

communion

sixteen

1 am the Lord your God in the midst of you. I am your *koinonia*, your fellowship, your communion, your participation, and your sharing. You can have no fellowship in Me unless you have it one with another. Your fellowship with one another, however, is in Me. You can have no fellowship with one another except you have it first in Me, for I am that which you have in common. Fellowship is having something in common in which you share, participate, and commune.

You come together in My name to participate in Me as My body, to share Me, and to share your lives one with another. This is part of what it means to come to the table of the Lord.

While eating the Passover supper with My chosen twelve on the night I was betrayed, I took the unleavened bread of Passover, gave thanks, broke it, and gave it to them saying, "This is My body which is given to you. This do in remembrance of Me." Likewise, I took the cup after supper and said, "This cup is the new testament in My blood, which is shed for you" *(Luke 22:21-20).* This was the cup of redemption. They had to drink from My cup. I could not drink from theirs.

Both the bread and wine were taken in remembrance of Me. They were to remember the blood sacrifice that I made for them on the cross. I was that Passover lamb of God *(Rev. 5:12).*

As I surrendered up My life, I made possible the restoration of My life for everyone who believes. Your sins were washed away that day. This forgiveness becomes a reality to you when you confess your sins and accept My forgiveness.

Then I told them, as I revealed to My servant Paul, that as often as they ate this bread and drank this cup they were proclaiming My death until I come again *(1 Cor. 11:23-26).*

There is more to this event than you have known in your institutional celebrations of "the Lord's supper." While it is a memorial of praise and celebration of My life, death, resurrection, and ascension, it is also a celebration of what it means to be My body—the body of Christ, My called-out-ones for assembly into Me.

It is your communion, your *koinonia.* Now that you believe, you are in Me and I am in you just as I and the Father are in one another. We share our lives together. You, too, have drunk from My cup. It is the cup of communion, fellowship, sharing, participation, and communication. You, too, have eaten of My flesh and drunk of My blood.

This is of particular importance because the life is in the blood *(Lev. 17:11).* I forbade the Israelites of old to drink the blood of animals because the life was in the blood. The animal sacrifices were a type and shadow [picture] of Me, but they were still animals. They could eat the flesh according to My law, but they were not to drink of any kind of life other than Mine.

Now that I have come in the fulfillment of these things that foreshadowed Me, you not only can drink My blood but you must drink of My blood if, indeed, you are to have My life. Yet, you cannot drink of My blood in the literal, physical sense; therefore, I have chosen the wine of the vine to represent this blood.

You eat of My body by taking your portion of My unleavened bread and eating it. Leaven is a type of sin and false teaching *(1 Cor. 5:6-9; Matt. 16:6,12).* There can be no leaven in the Passover bread *(Exod. 12:15).* The unleavened bread, therefore, represents My sinless life offered up for you as a ransom for your sin. You must understand this. Ask My Holy Spirit to reveal this truth to you in your spirit that you might walk in the light and reality of it.

The Corinthian believers did not understand this. When you show partiality among yourselves, when there is gossiping, back-biting, envy, and slandering among you, when there are divisions among you resulting from greed and power-positioning, you are drinking from your own cups. You are self-motivated gluttons.

When it was time for the Corinthians to take their meal together, they were not waiting on one another. If they were so hungry they could not wait upon each other to share their common meal together, they should have eaten at home before they came; but, because they did not rightly discern My body which they all had in common, they made a difference between themselves. It was not an *agape* feast [love-feast].[6] It was, instead a flesh feast. They were more caught up in feeding their own flesh than serving their brethren.

They did not know Me as they ought to have known Me. Had they known Me, they would have known that I would never put Myself first. I taught that the first—that is, those who lead—are last, and the last—that is, those who are led—are first. This is a Kingdom principle *(Mark 10:31).*

---

[6] It appears that the New Testament assemblies took their meals together in connection with the Lord's Supper. Jesus instituted His supper in the context of eating the Passover meal *(Matt. 26:26-30).* The Corinthians were obviously combining their common meal with the Lord's Supper. Paul addressed problems they were having with it *(1 Cor. 11:17-34).* NewTestament Christians called this their love-feast *(Jude 12).*

So you see, they were driven by their flesh. They did not discern My body; therefore, they were not celebrating Me. They were celebrating the idolatry of their own appetites. Their god was their belly *(Phil. 3:19)*. They, therefore, were eating and drinking in an unworthy manner. They were eating and drinking of themselves. When you do this, you end up devouring one another.

Now, for this reason, Paul rightly said to them, "Many are weak and sick, and many sleep [have died]." They needed to examine themselves, examine their motives for all the things they did. So also ought you. You who are self-invested persons will always find it difficult to express My body one to another. You must learn to discern your thoughts, attitudes, feelings, and lusts and divest yourself of self *(1 Cor. 11:27-30)*.

See how you are My body? This is My body; take, eat—that is, lay down your lives one for the other. Inasmuch as you begin to rightly discern My body in this way, I will come again to you and be the Presence in the midst of you. Until you learn what it means to be My body one to another, there will be no life, no power, and no presence. Divisions will always occur among you.

You have been called to a higher walk with Me. I invite you now to take communion with Me and do so until I come. In so drinking of the cup I have given you, you show My death until I come *(1 Cor. 11:26)*.

r e c e i v i n g

s e v e n t e e n

When you drink from My cup, you are given My life. You are given My cup. I give My life and My Spirit to you in measure. You now have that wine inside of you. Moreover, you have become the wine of who I am. You are Christians. Christ means anointed one. I am the anointed One of Israel. You are My anointed ones in that you have My anointing upon you.

Now that you have My wine in you and have become cups of My wine, I give you one to another as members of My body that you might drink from one another's cups. You are cups of life, power, healing, deliverance, praise, and worship—you are cups of blessing. Inasmuch as you willfully drink of one another's cups, you show the world who I really am. You show them My love, defined by My life. Have I not said that you shall know love by this, that one is willing to lay down his life for another (*John 15:13*)?

I have laid down My life that you might have My life. Now you are to lay down your lives that you might drink from one another's cups and have fullness of joy in Me. As you drink from one another's cups—receiving My ministries through one another—you increase My presence in the midst of you. Where My presence is, there is My glory.

My glory and My presence are what *koinonia* is all about. When you drink of My cup and eat of My bread you are partaking of My presence. Your communion, your fellowship is My presence.

Now, if you are to drink fully from Me, you must learn to receive the anointing I have put upon each of you in My body. This is what I meant when I said, "He who receives a prophet in the name of a prophet shall receive a prophet's reward; and he who receives a righteous man in the name of a righteous man shall receive a righteous man's reward" (*Matt. 10:41*). You receive the ministry benefits of the ministry that is given through that prophet and righteous man.

This is a Kingdom principle. Whenever you receive from the ministry or gift I have deposited upon others for your behalf, you are receiving from Me. You have to humble yourself of self-pride in order to do this.

When you do this, I release My anointing through them from whom you draw My life. This anointing flows through them to deliver the ministry or gift that you need. So, the ministry-gift that I have poured into other's cups is not for them, but for you. The ministry-gift that I have poured into your cup is not for you, but for others. Therefore, you are to drink from one another's cups which are portions from My common cup.

You are not to drink from your own cup. In the day you drink from your own cup, the wine is turned back into water. This is not the water of the word of God, but is the stagnate, defiled, polluted water of the flesh.

You are to discern the spirits and prove those who say they are apostles and prophets in your midst. If they come seeking something for self, they are false. If they come in the full surrender of self, they are true. They are true wine from the vine of I AM.

Therefore, test them to see if they bear My image. Do they labor to conform you into My image, or their own? Do they lay down their lives for you, or compel you to lay down your life for them? Do they point you to Me, or to their own works and ministries? Do they love authority in their own lives, or seek to rule with a heavy hand over your life? These are the kinds of questions you ask to discern whether men come in My name or in their own name.

Do not be deceived by their words. Rather, look at their fruit. Are they producing holy wine, or liquor for their wantonness? Do not receive from those who seek to enslave you, for the anointing upon them is not from Me but is the spirit of witchcraft, manipulation, control, deceit, and bondage.

Those who have learned what it means to lay down their lives one to another, who prefer others over themselves, who submit one to another are My true servants. You can receive from them and be fed the good grass from My pastures. I am the Good Shepherd. I love My sheep and lay down My life for them. So it is with My shepherds.

Watch out for those in your midst who try to put you under the law. They spy out your liberty. They are the enemies of My grace. Do not receive from them, rather run from them. They have no part in you and you have no part in them, just as I have no part in them and they have no part in Me. I cannot fellowship in a legalistic atmosphere. Where My Spirit is, there is liberty (*2 Cor. 3:17*).

I have come to heal you, deliver you, set you free, and save you from your sins. Receive from Me through one another in the portions of My life I have given you. Receive the prophet in the name of a prophet and you will receive the prophet's reward— you will receive the rewards of the prophet's anointing. You will receive My presence, My power, My life, My glory. I desire more than anything to be the Presence in the midst of you.

o b e d i e n c e

e i g h t e e n

$\mathcal{1}$ am the Presence in your midst. I am the anointing that is upon you. I am the ministry and the gift of the Spirit that is within you. You are My body, My hands, My feet, My eyes, My ears, My mouth, My heart. You are My word, My will, My way made manifest in the world. Because I live, you live. Because I love, you love. Because I obeyed, you obey.

My people, those who are called by My name, are an obedient people. They love Me; that is, they would lay down their lives for Me. Therefore, they would lay down their lives for one another. They are an obedient people. What they see Me doing, they do. What they hear Me saying, they say. Where they see Me going, they go.

They have no regard for their own lives. They have no fear of what others will think of them. They are dead on their feet. That is what it takes to be a radically obedient people. They love not their own lives unto the death. Therefore, they have overcome the wicked one *(Rev. 12:11)*.

They do not love the world nor the things in the world because My love is in them. They have no part in that which is in the world: the lust of the flesh, the lust of the eyes, and the pride of life. They know that these things are not of Me but are of the world *(1 John 2:15-16)*. They are those who will follow Me wherever I go *(Rev. 14:4)*. They are those who are faithful in the little things, that I might put them in charge of the greater things *(Matt. 25:21)*.

It is, therefore, imperative that each of you understand how important it is for you to obey Me in everything. As you obey Me in all things, you will do the things pertaining to the anointing that is upon you.

Remember, you are sharing Me when you move in your anointing. You are being a cup of blessing when you move in your anointing. The ministry and the gift that are upon you and in you are not about you, but are all about Me. Set aside your self-consciousness and risk doing the things I say for you to do. Move out in faith. Stir up the gifts within you, knowing that you are ministering My life and My power, not yours. You are administering Me, not yourself.

Obey Me faithfully and you will become the ministry and the gift I have placed in you. Failure to move out in obedience robs others of the life and blessing I wish to impart to them. Humble yourselves and obey. Pride and ego keep you from faithfulness. Obedience releases My power, and where My power is, there is My presence.

Obey Me in the little things and I can later put you in charge of the greater. The little obediences are for your training.

First comes the call. You were called from before the foundation of the earth, but the call is not the function. The call has to be cast into the crucible of preparation. Because of this, I require that My sons and daughters go through their personal wildernesses. Each wilderness experience is intended to take you out of Egypt [the world] and take Egypt out of you.

Do not dread My wilderness. Great and glorious things happen in the wilderness. I plant My word in your heart and sustain you miraculously as I lead you to the fulfillment of your destiny—the promised land.

Thus, after your wilderness time has been fulfilled, you will come out of your wilderness as I came out of Mine in the power of My Spirit *(Luke 4:14)*. My anointing will come upon you. You will know when this anointing comes upon you. You will then be empowered to do the greater things you were called to do.

With the anointing comes authority. You have authority from Me to be who I have made you to be. I am the highest authority in all the universe. I place authority upon whom I will. You have the authority to operate in the ministry or gift I have placed within you. You do not have authority to do or be anything else.

You have different gifts according to the grace that I have given to you. If you have been given prophecy, then prophesy according to the proportion of the faith; if ministry, then minister; if teaching, then teach; if exhortation, then exhort; if giving, then give; if ruling, then rule with diligence; if mercy, then show it with cheerfulness. Do what I have given you to do with simplicity (*Rom. 12:6-8*).

Each of you have ministries and gifts. With these ministries and gifts come the anointings and the authority. Recognize who has what ministry and what gift and submit to the anointing and authority of that ministry or gift. Each person has authority in your life only in terms of their ministry and gifting. This authority operates only as long as their ministry and gifting operates.

It behooves each of you to submit to My word for you in one another. Submission is joyfully entered into voluntarily. It cannot be coerced. You are free and must allow everyone else to be free. Submission to authority is a matter of the heart. You are either submitted or not. Oppression does not yield submission.

True submission, then, is the simple act of receiving the gift of Me through the agency of another member of My body. When you submit to the ministry and gift for you through another member of the body, you are submitting unto Me. I am that ministry and that gift. When you release your ministry and your gift, you are releasing Me to say and do what I desire to say and do to build up My body. The ministries and gifts of the Spirit are given for the sole purpose of building up My body into Me.

When My ministries and My gifts are freely released and received by each of you, I become the Presence in the midst of you. We share and participate in one another; we have communion and fellowship one with another. We are one body and I am the head of it *(Eph. 1:22-23)*.

In such a time as this, the truth of Paul's words to the Ephesians becomes a living, dynamic reality: You are indeed keeping the unity of the Spirit in the bond of peace. You are one body and one Spirit just as you are called in one hope of your calling. You have one Lord, one faith, one baptism, one God and Father of you all, who is above all, and through all, and in you all *(Eph. 4:3-6)*. You have true *koinonia* and I am the Presence in the midst of you.

Above all things have fervent love among yourselves, for love covers a multitude of sins. Use hospitality one to another without grudging. As every man received the gift, even so minister the same to one another as good stewards of the manifold grace of God. If you speak, speak My words. If you minister, minister by the ability which I have given you that I might be glorified in all things *(1 Pet. 4:8-11)*.

B *e*

n i n e t e e n

*M*inistries and giftings are not what you do. They are who you are according to the anointing that is upon you. You have only to do who you are. Ministry has far more to do with being than with doing.

The gifts and callings are without repentance *(Rom. 11:29)*. I do not change My mind and take them away. This is how I formed you in My mind before the foundation of the earth. If I were to change your gifting and calling, I would have to change who you are.

I have chosen you to be exactly who you are, to be the part of

Me I have given you to be. You do not have to have a name for it. You do not have to hang your identity on it. Just be who you are and do what you do and your gifts will make room for you (*Prov. 18:16*).

You fail to understand true ministry when you ambitiously seek it for yourself. You cannot seek it, for it is who you are in Me. You fail to understand true ministry when you try to legitimize it as an entity outside of yourself. You cannot incorporate who you are in Me. If that which you call ministry can be legally incorporated in the world system, it is not the real thing. You are the real thing. You are Me. You do not need to advertise it, promote it, solicit funds for it, and get others to join it. You simply need to function in who you are in Me as I lead you by My Holy Spirit (*Rom. 8:14*).

You are your ministry. I have made you to be who you are. If you will only see that I have need of you to be Me in special ways to others, you will be free of these trappings that professional ministry straps on you.

Be who I have made you to be. Say what you hear Me say. Do what you see Me doing as it pertains to your life, no matter how small or large the task may seem. Be who I have made you to be, and you will complete My joy.

You do not need "your ministry" to make you feel okay with Me. I need you to be Me as I lead. Mostly, I want only to be in your midst. I want the pleasure of your company.

I assure you, as I live and breathe upon you, that if you will spend time with Me, completing My joy, you will be all of who I have made you to be.

See, I am the anointing upon you. I go where you go. I do according to the anointing upon you. I don't always even need for you to say or do anything. Just be willing to take Me where I want to go so I can be the Presence in that situation and do what I desire to do.

When you come together to worship and praise Me, you bring that unique part of Me in you into your gatherings. You usher in My presence. My collective presence in each of you allows Me to be and do what I choose to be and do in your midst.

Therefore, when you come together, allow Me to operate. Lay aside your own agendas, traditions, and patterns. Be willing to wait upon Me. Be still and know that I am God *(Ps. 46:10)*. Rest. Wait. Listen. Then, do.

Do only what I ask you to do. Do not add to or take away from what I require of you. Simply trust and obey.

p e r f e c t e d

t w e n t y

*B*e therefore perfect, even as your heavenly Father who is in heaven is perfect" *(Matt. 5:48)*. I alone am perfecting a people who will show forth My glory, My presence, in this hour before My coming. I have ordained that it be so from before the foundations of the earth. I will have sons, patterned after My Son, Jesus Christ, who will be brought to glory—manifested even before I come.

Many of you will find this offensive because you think and teach these things as fleshly men. You have devised doctrines surrounding My second coming that do not agree with the whole counsel of My word.

You have devised your own impressions of what My coming again looks like. I say to you that My disciples—those who walked by My side in the earth and heard Me teach in the physical and speak of Kingdom things—did not know what Passover looked like until I fulfilled it on the cross. They did not know what Pentecost looked like until I fulfilled it on the day of Pentecost.

I poured out My Spirit at Pentecost and bore witness to them by My Spirit that this was that which Joel had said would happen. My servant Peter explained to them then, "And it shall come to pass in the last days...I will pour out of My Spirit upon all flesh. And your sons and your daughters shall prophesy, and your young men shall see visions, and your old men shall dream dreams. And on My servants and on my handmaidens I will pour out in those days of My Spirit, and they shall prophesy. And I will show wonders in heaven above and signs in the earth beneath: blood, and fire, and vapor of smoke" *(Acts 2:17-19)*.

Even then I spoke through Peter, and he heard it said himself for the first time, that I will have yet the fulfillment of My final feast—the feast of Tabernacles. When Peter added from Joel these words, "the sun shall be turned into darkness and the moon into blood before that great and notable day of the Lord comes. And it shall come to pass that whosoever shall call on the name of the Lord shall be saved" *(Acts 2:20-21)*, he went beyond Pentecost looking forward to the end of Pentecost which is Tabernacles.

You are now hearing My trumpets blow. Blow the trumpet in Zion, I say. Sound the alarm in My holy mountain. Let all the inhabitants of the land tremble, for the day of the Lord comes, for it is near at hand *(Joel 2:1)*.

My trumpet is My wake up call. "Awake sleeper. Arise from the dead. And Christ will shine on you" *(Eph. 5:14 NAS)*. Wake up from being at ease in Zion *(Amos 6:1)*. Rise up and come out to Me that I might cleanse you, perfect you, and bring forth My army of holy and sanctified sons.

You ask, how can this be? How can we possibly be perfected before you come? You think as fleshly men and women. You think your perfection lies within your hands. How so when your salvation was not in your hands, but in Mine? You think falsely that you can perfect yourself in your own strength.

See, I send My messenger who will prepare the way before Me. I, whom you seek, will suddenly come to My temple...But who can endure the day of My coming? Who can stand when I appear? I am like a refiner's fire and like fullers' soap. I will sit as a refiner and purifier of silver. I will purify the sons of Levi and purge them as gold and silver that they may offer to Me an offering of righteousness (*Mal. 3:1-3*), that they may be righteous, even as I am righteous.

I am bringing My true sons to maturity just as I said I would in Ephesians 4:11-13. I give gifts to men. I give some to be apostles, some prophets, some evangelists, some pastors and teachers. These are given to equip the saints for the work of service until all of you become one man. I am bringing you to the unity of the faith. This has not yet happened. I am bringing you to the knowledge of the Son of God. This has not yet fully happened. I am bringing you to a perfect man. This has not yet happened. I am bringing you to the measure of the stature of the fullness of Christ. This has not yet happened, but it is happening now.

In that day of My appearing, you shall be like Me (*1 John 3:2*), because, as I am, so are you in this world (*1 John 4:17*). My Father is bringing many sons to glory before I come. It was fitting for Him who made all things, for all things are from Him, in bringing many sons to glory, to make the captain of their salvation perfect through sufferings (*Heb 2:10-11*).

My glory is My presence. My presence is My glory. When My presence is made manifest in the midst of you, repentance falls upon you, righteousness reigns over you. Your old man of flesh cannot stand in My presence. My oil of anointing is poured out upon you. I am separating you today from your sin, your flesh, the world, and the domain of Satan to fill you with My glory; that is, My presence. It is no longer you who live, but Me who lives in you; and the life you now live in the flesh, you live according to My faith in you. I am the one who loved you and gave My life up for you (*Gal. 2:20*).

Do not be dismayed by the idea that I might bring My sons to glory before I come. Why not? I can do as I please. It is My good pleasure to do so, but you must fully understand it is not about you. It is about Me. I will bring Myself to glory. I will so fill My house, My temple with My presence that the whole earth will tremble at the sight of Me.

Twice before, My glory filled the temple. The first was in the tabernacle of Moses. That tabernacle was a type of Me with the

Outer Court of the feast of Passover, the Holy Place of the feast of Pentecost, the Most Holy Place of the feast of Tabernacles. These courts and feasts correspond to one another and tell of times and seasons in Me. The second time My glory filled the temple was at the completion of Solomon's temple which was built exactly as I had prescribed (1 Kings 6-8). My glory fills the house that I make according to the pattern that I give. Unless I build My house, those who build, build in vain (Ps. 127:1). The third and final time that My glory shall fill the temple is soon to come to My people who build according to My pattern—the fulfillment of Tabernacles.

You are now coming into the fulfillment of this feast of Tabernacles, or shall I say, Tabernacles is coming upon you; that is, those of you who are ready and willing to have your lamps filled with the oil of My Holy Spirit.

Yes. I AM is coming for the third and final time to fill My temple, of whom you are, with My Spirit in the fullness of My presence and My glory.

You will be glorified because I am your glorification. It is not you who are being perfected. It is Me, the perfect, who is perfected in you, upon you, and through you.

I am the glory of Israel. The Presence of the most holy and high God. There is no other besides Me. Seek Me with a whole heart. Walk only after Me and I shall show you yet an ever better and higher way.

AUTHORITY

twenty-one

The anointing that is upon you is My ministry through you. You are the vehicle of My presence. Therefore I say to you,

"Go...and teach all nations, baptizing them in the name of the Father, and of the Son, and of the Holy Ghost; teaching them to observe all things whatsoever I have commanded you. And lo, I am with you always, even to the completion of the age" (*Matt. 28:19-20*).

"I am with you" speaks not only to those then, but to all who are called by My name "to the completion of the age." Now as never before I am increasing and intensifying My presence in the midst of you that each of you might go out in My name and collectively do greater works than even I did (*John 14:12*).

See, the lame walk, the blind see, the deaf hear, and the dead are raised from the grave. You shall do these and greater works than these. I will pour out fire from heaven through you at My command. I will hold back the rain when it should be raining. I will cause it to snow when it is impossible to snow. I will do all My wonders—just as I did in the days of Moses and Aaron in Egypt—that the world may know Me and know that you, My glorified sons, have come in the name of the Lord.

You will bless who I bless and curse who I curse. You will heal who I heal and afflict who I afflict. You will be rods of judgment in My hand and say what you hear Me saying and do what you see Me doing (*Ps. 2:9; Rev. 2:27; 12:5*).

I am increasing My presence, My glory in the world, and I choose to do it through My holy ones, My remnant in the world.

Wherever you go, you bear the brand mark of the cross on your forehead. It is not a brand mark made with human hands, but is an invisible mark put there by your lifestyle. You take Me with you. You take Me where I want to go. You take the special anointing of Me upon you to the people and places to whom and where I want to go.

When you who are anointed of Me come together by My Spirit, there will be a multiplication of My presence that exceeds the simple sum of your collective presence. You will draw from one another and impart to one another the anointings of Me upon you all. Back and forth. The individual anointing upon you will increase as you partake of the anointing upon the other. You will feed your anointings to one another as you prophesy over one another and impart blessings upon one another.

This is how I equip the saints for the work of service. These are tools you cannot acquire in workshops. Stay sensitive to My Spirit whenever you are with other brothers and sisters that you might impart the blessing of who I am in you to them.

Failure to act on My word when you know you have My word for another is arrogance and self-centeredness. Repent from ever thinking My gifting upon you has anything to do with you. You are no more special with an anointing for ministry upon you than you are without it. Therefore, do not think more highly of yourself than you ought to think, but think soberly, according to the measure of faith I have dealt to every man *(Rom. 12:3)*.

Now as you partake of Me through one another's anointing, you are having communion in the truest, purest sense of the word.

If you understand this, that My supper is My presence and My presence is My supper, you rightly discern My body; and if you understand that My presence is My anointing upon you and you are to eat and drink of Me through one another, then you rightly discern My body.

Therefore, eat My body and drink My blood that you may increase in My presence and power, that you may take My presence and power to the uttermost parts of the earth. Go where I go.

All authority has been given to Me by My Father *(Matt. 18:18b)*. I give this authority to you. First comes the call to ministry. Then comes the time of preparation by My Holy Spirit for that ministry. In due season, My anointing for that calling falls upon you. With that anointing comes the mantle of authority.

All authority has been given to Me. I hereby impart this authority to you for the anointing that is upon you. The anointing that is upon you is My ministry through you.

Do not become faint of heart in your wilderness of preparation for I have promised never to leave you nor forsake you *(Heb. 13:5)*.

Be steadfast and of good cheer. Know that the anointing upon you is now increasing and separating you from all that is in and of the world.

the final
CALL

twenty - two

All I want is to indwell My people and to be your dwelling place. I want to be your habitation. I want to love you, feed you, nurture you, comfort you, strengthen you, heal you, and bring you into My holiness. I want to delight in you, rejoice with you, dance and dine with you, and you with Me.

Many of My people, even those I have called, are stubborn and obstinate. They want to fellowship in their own willful ways more than in Mine. Look at them. Look at those who have grown old in their rejection of Me. There is no life in their countenance, no light in their eyes. They have turned away from abiding in Me and have chosen to abide in themselves. Their own rejection of Me has caused their hearts to be turned to stone. They have stone faces, sculptured by the deceit of their own hearts. I have now rejected them because they have rejected Me. They have so hardened their own hearts against Me that there is no place for repentance left in them.

Therefore, by the power of My wrath, I have taken My hand off of them and I am causing My great judgments to fall upon them. My wrath is revealed from heaven against all ungodliness and unrighteousness of men who hold the truth in unrighteousness, because that which may be known of Me is revealed in them, for I have showed it to them (*Rom. 1:19*). My judgments are righteous.

You in your soulish heart ask, "What kind of a God is that?" I am a God of love. I have already poured forth My great, unfathomable love toward you all. Many of you have rejected Me. It was not I who rejected you. Yet in rejecting Me you cause My wrath to spring forth. You denied My great sacrifice of love toward you.

I died for you that you might live, that you might have My kind of life. Many of you choose death. Death is the absence of My life. Where My life is, there is peace and joy. Where My life is absent, there is death and destruction.

You who have rejected the precious wooing of My Holy Spirit have rejected Me. Time after time I showed mercy toward you for your sin. I overlooked your obstinacy. I beckoned you to come unto Me, to love Me, obey Me, dwell with Me and allow Me to dwell with you. I am a patient God, long-suffering. I am full of grace, mercy, and kindness toward you.

You are no better than My chosen ones, Israel. I continued to send My prophets to her to call her out of her idolatrous ways, for she was committing spiritual harlotry right in My own house, My temple, the place of My presence in the midst of them. They did not repent. In due time, in the fullness of time, I rejected her. I divorced her and exiled her to her Assyrian lovers (Jer. 3:8). Yes, I say to you, you are no better than she.

This is once again, the fullness of time. You are coming into the end of an era. Now is the hour of your salvation. Choose Me this day for the night is quickly coming. The call will fade away, the trumpeters will sound no more. Your redemption is near you now.

Listen to My Holy Spirit. Listen to My prophet. Renounce your willful ways. Abandon all that is in your hearts that cause you to turn away from Me. This is your final call.

Oh, how I long once more to spread My wings over you, to nestle you to My breast, but many of you, in your rebellion, wiggle out of My arms and run to do your own thing.

This time, My beloved, I have determined to let go those of you who are unrepentant. You have chosen your own way, but it is not My way (Rom. 1:28-32). You see, I am My way. I am the way, the truth, and the life. No man comes to the Father except through Me (John 14:6).

Come to Me in faithfulness and trust. Abide in Me and let Me abide in you. I desire nothing more than to be the Presence in the midst of you, to dine with you, to drink the cup of blessing with you. Come, My beloved. Come quickly, come now. Don't look back. Love not the world nor the things in the world. If you love the world and the things in the world, those things will be your God. They will possess you far more than you will possess them.

Are you able? Are you willing? Will you abandon these things in your heart and run to Me with a whole heart? Will you allow Me to wash you white as snow, to dress you in fine linen, to take you into My chamber as My bride, to sit you at the head of My banquet table with Me?

Do you feel My heart? My love? My compassion? The greater My love is for you, the greater My wrath is provoked within Me toward those who defy and reject My wooing.

This is the final act. The curtain is closing. The bows are taking place. To whom will you bow, to self, or to Me, the Lord God Almighty, maker of heaven and earth?

Come!

Come quickly!

Come now!

Allow Me to be the Presence in the midst of you.

the ARK

twenty-three

Come with Me, My people. Let Me show you My heart. Let Me show you how very much I am the Presence in the midst of you.

I was with you in Egypt when I saw your desperation. I met with My servant Moses on Mount Horeb and commissioned him to go and say to Pharaoh, "Let My people go." I was with him there and with his brother Aaron. I was the power in the rod that turned the water to blood and sent the frogs and lice and flies. I was the power that diseased the livestock and sent the boils and the hail and the locusts and the darkness. I was the death angel and the Passover lamb and the blood on the lintels of your door posts. I was the unleavened bread and the cloud by day and the pillar of fire by night *(Exod. 3-13)*.

I was the Presence that divided the waters of the Red Sea that you might pass over on dry ground. I was the Presence that allowed your enemy to drown that you might see My salvation and My deliverance, for I, the Lord your God fight your battles for you *(Exod. 14:13-14)*.

Despite your murmurings and grumblings, I was the wilderness through which you were made to pass. I was the tree Moses cast into the bitter water at Marah that made it sweet for you to drink, and I was the water *(Exod. 15:22-25; Rev. 22:2)*. I was the bread, the manna, that came down out of heaven to sustain you all the days of your wilderness journey *(Exod. 16; John 6:57-58)*. I was the rock of Massah and Meribah and the water that came forth from that rock that you might drink and not be thirsty *(Exod. 17:1-7; I Cor.10:4)*.

I was the Presence on Mount Sinai where I gave My law to My servant Moses that you might all know Me and know My heart, that I might create for you boundaries of safekeeping if you would only obey My words *(Exod. 20)*.

You were afraid of My presence—the thunder, the lightning, the trumpet, and the smoking mountain. You trembled and drew back from Me. You wanted Moses to speak to Me instead of hearing My voice for yourself. You thought in your heart that if you heard My voice, you would certainly die *(Exod. 20:18-19)*. I spoke to you through My servant Moses that you might know My heart and long in your heart to trust and obey Me.

I gave you the portion of My feasts and My tabernacle. I made a provision for you in the natural whereby you might experience My presence in the supernatural.

You made the ark of My testimony for Me as I prescribed that I might have a place to dwell in the midst of you. I had you to make it out of acacia wood which represented My earthly existence among you; yet, I had you to overlay it with pure gold to represent My deity. You cast four rings of gold and put them on each corner of My ark that you might carry Me about with you on sanctified shoulders. There, in the wilderness, I had you put the testimony into My ark. You made a mercy seat and two cherubim of gold to rest on either side. Their outstretched wings hovered over the mercy seat as they faced one another. There I promised to meet with you *(Exod. 25:1-22)*.

The ark of the testimony was the ark of My presence. After you completed the tabernacle according to the pattern I gave you in the wilderness, you brought the ark of My presence into the Most Holy Place, behind the veil *(Exod. 26:33)*.

I wanted to be the Presence in the midst of you, but you were a stiff-necked people. I could have come up into your midst in one moment and consumed you *(Exod. 33:5)*. Rather, My servant Moses pitched his tent, separated himself from you outside the camp, and called his tent the tabernacle of meeting. Those who had a Moses heart, who sought My presence, went out to where he was *(Exod. 33:7)*.

I assure you that I, once again, will raise up a Moses people who will love My presence enough to separate themselves from the harlotry of the people, to go outside of the camp and be a tabernacle for Me. I will be a pillar of cloud descending upon them. I will talk with them. They will be the ark of My presence. My presence will go with them and I will give them rest *(Exod. 33:14)*.

I separated a people of praise, the Levites, to bear the ark of My presence and to stand before Me to minister to Me and to bless My name. I was their inheritance *(Deut. 10:8-9)*.

I will not be touched by defiled hands. When My presence is carried about on sanctified shoulders—the shoulders of self-denial and obedience—I bring forth all My good blessings and prosperity. The land prospers and diseases are healed. When hands touch Me that have been defiled by the rebellion and stubbornness of unbelief and transgressions, I bring forth famine, disease, and death. My presence is an awesome force. It is a two-edged sword, piercing the righteous for good and the unrighteous for evil.

The ark of My presence went out before you while you were still in My wilderness. I went out before you for three days searching out a resting place for you. My cloud was above you by day when you went out from the camp. Moses would say whenever My ark went out from you, "Rise up, O Yahweh, let your enemies be scattered." When it rested he said, "Return, O Yahweh, to the many thousands of Israel" *(Num. 10:33-36)*.

Again I say, I will have a Moses people who will follow My ark when they see Me going out before them and will rest when they see Me resting. I will have a people who will enter into My rest *(Heb. 4:1-11)*. The ark of My presence was the power that held back the Jordan for you to pass over into My land of promise *(Josh. 3)*. The ark of My presence was the power that caused the walls of Jericho to fall *(Josh 6)*.

I was sorely grieved, however, when you brought the ark of My presence into your midst to fight battles I had not declared. You tried to use Me for your own gain against the armies of the Philistines and you were sorely defeated. I was taken away captive by the very enemy I sought to destroy before you. You went up before Me. You did not wait for Me to go up before you.

Learn the lesson at Ebenezer. My ark is My presence. When I am present, My glory reigns. My presence and My glory are one. On that day when it was said, "The ark of God was captured," Eli fell back, broke his neck and died. Hophni and Phinehas, his two sons, sons of rebellion and grief, also died that day. My glory departed Israel because My ark had been captured. Ichabod [which means "no glory"] was born *(1 Sam. 4)*.

I was taken to Ashdod and put side by side with the abomination of the Philistine god, Dagon, as if I could share My glory with another. My presence knocked it on its face. Even a second time I struck it down and cut off its head and palms, for these represent the idolatry of the imaginations of men and the works of their hands.

Twice My hand was heavy upon the people of Ashdod. I ravaged and struck them with tumors. I was not to remain with them. You cannot defile the glory of My presence. They carried Me away to Gath and I struck that city with tumors. Then, they sent Me to Ekron. The Philistines counseled together and agreed that I should go back to My own place because My wrath was kindled against Ekron as well *(1 Sam. 5)*.

The ark of My presence was the power that guided the cow-drawn cart from their midst to its resting place at Beth-shemesh *(1 Sam. 6:1-16)*. The ark of My presence was the power that struck the men of Beth-shemesh dead because they dared to look into My presence out of curiosity *(1 Sam 6:19)*. Men who look into My face for the sake of their kingdoms shall never see My glory. The men of Kiriah-jearim brought Me into the house of Abinadab. They consecrated Eleazar to keep the ark of My presence *(1 Sam. 7:1)*, I remained there until My servant David sought to bring Me up to his appointed place. He tried to bring Me up on a cart of his own making, but I can only be carried about on sanctified shoulders *(2 Sam. 6:2-7)*.

The ark is My presence in the midst of you. My presence is My work in your lives. Do not touch what I am doing. Do not start what I have not started. Do not try to stop what I have started. Do not add on to what I am doing. Do not take away from what I am doing. Do not touch My presence in the lives of others to try to alter it, to judge or criticize them. They are My workmanship, not yours.

I remained in the house of Obed-Edom for three months whereupon I blessed him and all his household *(2 Sam. 6:10-11)*. My presence brings blessings to those who bless Me and are willing for Me to tabernacle with them.

David later brought the ark of My presence to the city of David with gladness. He danced before Me with all his might. They brought Me up with shouting and with the sound of the trumpet *(2 Sam. 6:12-15)*. So shall I be brought into your midst. I indeed inhabit the praises of Israel *(Ps. 22:3)*. You are My Israel.

You brought the ark of My presence and set it in its place in the midst of the tabernacle that David had erected for Me (*2 Sam. 6:17*).

I was the Presence in the midst of you in Moses' tabernacle, in David's tabernacle, and in Solomon's temple (*1 Kings 8*). When the priests had placed Me in the Most Holy Place of Solomon's temple and came out from there, My glory cloud filled My house. The priests who ministered there could not continue because of My glory, My presence. Oh, how I long to be the Presence in the midst of you.

You defiled My temple, My dwelling place. Time and again you brought your gods of power and sex into My Holy Place. I departed your presence. I cannot, I will not bless your flesh and your idolatries with My presence. Rather, you invited for yourself gods of deception. You were deluded.

The ark of My presence was no longer found on earth after King Nebuchadnezzar destroyed My house and took away My people, Judah, into captivity. You rebelled against Me and would not repent.

Men search for Me, the ark of Jehovah, hoping to find a great treasure—an astounding, invaluable archeological find. They will not find it here, for I have hidden it in heaven. It shall be seen when My temple in heaven is opened. Once again, on that day, as it was with Moses on Mount Sinai, there shall be lightning, noises, thunderings, an earthquake, and great hail (*Rev. 11:19*).

My ark is no longer to be found made of acacia wood overlaid with gold in its natural form, but is to be found in the heart and lives of all who are called by My name, all who believe in Me for whom the ark was a representation. I am that covenant of stone that has been put in the ark of human hearts that I might have a temple of living stones.

In these last days, I am appearing, even now, to rebuild the tabernacle of David which has fallen down. I will rebuild its ruins and set it up, so that the rest of mankind may seek Me (*Acts 15:16-17*).

My glory shall return to My temple a third time. I will come to you, the temple of My Holy Spirit. I will come to My glorified sons and daughters. My presence is My glory, My Spirit.

the many

The next great move of My Spirit upon the face of the earth will be the manifestation of My glory upon My sons and daughters in My kingdom.

I shall come upon you, My sons and daughters, My obedient ones. I shall come upon you in the power of My presence, and where I am there is My glory, My presence. Just as I have been in you and you in Me, now I shall manifest Myself more fully upon you.

I have visited key places in recent years, but I am about to move from places to people. I will not just hover over a place, for men venerate places. I will not just hover over a few men, for men venerate men. I will, instead, hover over the nameless, faceless many who will carry My glory about wherever they go. They will go where I say go.

As it was in the beginning so shall it be in the end. I shall have sons and daughters who bear My image, who are conformed unto Me, the pattern son, who reflect My glory, the glory of the Father. I have been glorified by the Father and am being glorified in you (*John 13:31; 17:10*).

Now hear this, all you who seek My face, all you who desire to go the distance with Me. The call goes out from Me, even in this letter to you. I am calling you, even inviting you to sit with

Me at My table, for the wedding of the Lamb and His bride is about to take place.

I have likened you and My kingdom to ten of you virgins who took your lamps and went out to meet Me, the bridegroom (*Matt. 25*). Five of you were wise and five of you were foolish. Ten is the number of the measure of human responsibility. You had a responsibility and the opportunity to answer My call, to obey Me, to allow Me to lead you in My upward way. Therefore, I sent My Holy Spirit, that you might be led of Him. Where I go, He goes. If any man desires to follow Me, he must obey the leading of My Holy Spirit in all things. Those who are led by My Spirit are My true sons (*Rom. 8:14*).

Ten divided by two equals five. Five is My number for grace. I extend the call and I give the grace to answer the call. You have "response-ability" to heed My call because My grace is sufficient (*2 Cor. 12:9*). I shall never violate your free will. Thus, five of you frustrated My grace and did not prepare yourselves to go the distance with Me.

Two is My number for witness and corporateness. You are My witnesses in the world. I shall make a difference between you and the world. Men shall look upon you and see the glory I have manifested upon you and know that I am real, that I am God. I shall no longer be sought after by the power of men's intellect, but by the manifestation of My power and My Spirit (*Zech. 4:6*). I will not be known by your speech and persuasive preaching of human wisdom, but in demonstration of My Spirit and power, that the faith of others shall not be in the wisdom of men, but in My power (*1 Cor. 2:4-5*). Just as ten is divided by two, so shall I make a separation between the sons of men and My sons of glory, between the faithless and the faithful, the disobedient and the obedient.

Five of you were foolish because you did not take oil with you. You had lamps with wicks sufficient to go the distance, but you ignored My word to be filled with My Holy Spirit that you might have the power of My lordship in your life. You tried to light your own lamps with your own wisdom, doctrines, and pathetic guidance. You tried to perfect yourselves by your own laws, rules, and regulations.

Nevertheless, five of you were wise for you took oil with you for your lamps. Oil is a type of My Holy Spirit. Without the oil of My Holy Spirit you have no light within you, you have no anointing upon you. You must heed My word and fill the lamp of your lives with the precious oil of My Holy Spirit.

I have given all of you enough time to purchase this oil for yourselves. Many of you are growing weary of waiting for Me. You thought I would come at the setting of the sun, at the beginning of a new day. No! That was the time of My burial, a time of mourning. I delayed. Just as I delayed going to Lazarus after he had been dead and entombed for three days (John 11:1-44), so am I delaying through the early hours of the night. Many of you are not watchful, but have grown weary in the wait. You, like Peter after My crucifixion, decided to go fishing (John 21:3).

Then, at the midnight hour, when all hope had drained from the spirits of the unbelieving five virgins, My cry sounded. "The bridegroom comes. Go out to meet Him" (Matt. 25:6).

All of you arose and trimmed your lamps. You who had not purchased for yourselves the extra baptism in My Spirit found yourselves wanting. You expected others to give you what they had. They could not. Their anointing had been walked out through past obediences.

The five wise virgins had sought Me early. They desired to know My will and to walk faithfully in My way and My word. They cultivated obedience. They had practiced obeying Me in the little things so that now they would have the oil of faithfulness for the one great thing.

My Holy Spirit has been given to you to testify of Me (John 15:26); to convict the world of sin, righteousness, and judgment (John 16:8); to guide you into all truth (John 16:13); to glorify Me (John 16:14); and to give you My ability to be My witnesses in all the world (Acts 1:8). He is the necessary oil in My lamp. You purchase oil by the sacrifice of your own will and ways, by laying down your life in return for a life of obedience to Me.

Believe Me, when I tell you, the times are coming soon when a great darkness will cover the earth. It will be the midnight of your lives. Many of you who have looked for Me through false visions and doctrines will lose faith and falter. You need not do so. Begin now to seek Me with a whole heart, abandon everything else in your heart, get quiet before Me, learn to hear My voice, practice obedience. Let Me train you through exercise how to obey Me. Even I learned obedience through the things I suffered (*Heb. 5:8*). Obedience is the mark of true sonship.

My oil is My Holy Spirit. My lamp is your temple, for you are the temple of the Holy Spirit. Your spirit is the wick and I am the light of the world. You, too, are lights. Do not wait until you hear My cry to try to purchase the oil of obedience from others. You will have to go back to purchase it; that is, to practice obedience to My Holy Spirit. While you are gone, I will have come and those who were ready will go into My wedding with Me and the door will shut behind Me.

You will come later, knock, and cry, "Lord, Lord, open to us."

I will say, "I do not know you. You call Me Lord, but you did not obey Me. How then could I be your Lord? I am Lord to those who faithfully obey Me."

Watch therefore, for you do not know the day nor the hour when I, the Son of man, come (*Matt. 25:10-13*).

I am bringing many sons to glory (*Heb. 2:10*). These are they who are faithful and true—obedient sons of the living God. They are the ones upon whom I shall pour out My Spirit, My presence, My glory. My glory will not come and go but will come and abide upon them. I will be their pillar of fire by night and their cloud by day. I shall feed them manna on a daily basis. I shall plant My covenant firmly within the ark of their lives. They shall know Me from the rising to the setting of the sun. I shall scatter them to the far corners of the earth by the wind of My Holy Spirit. They shall be Me as I go forth, revealing My glory to all men everywhere. I am and always will be the Presence in the midst of them.

They are Melchizedeks who have no beginning nor end, no genealogy except in Me. They offer the bread and the wine of My sacrificed life (*Heb, 7:1-3; Gen. 14:18*). They, too, shall live the cross of Christ. I am their portion, their provision. They are My presence in the midst of you. Eat, drink, and be satisfied, for I am the bread of life *(John 6:35,48)* and the water of life. If any man drinks of Me, he shall never thirst again *(John 4:14)*.

f u l l n e s s

t w e n t y - f i v e

*I*n My presence is fullness of joy *(Ps. 16:11)*.

How much of My presence do you want? Thirtyfold measure, sixtyfold measure, or a hundredfold measure *(Matt. 13:8)*? It is your choice. I invite you to come into the fullness of Me, to tabernacle with Me.

There are three courts to My tabernacle. The Outer Court, the Holy Place, and the Most Holy Place. You must go through the Outer Court to come into the Holy Place, and you must come into the Holy Place before you can go on into the Most Holy Place. I invite you to come into the Most Holy Place, into the fullness of Me.

When you come to the Outer Court, you come to My Passover. You come to My crucifixion—the cross—whereupon I yielded My life and poured out My blood, gave up My body that you might have My life eternal.

Come! Drink of this cup. Eat My body. Drink My blood. Be born again. Be raised into new life and ascend upon high. Sit in the heavenlies with Me. That is your destiny, to be with Me and I with you.

Come on in, My precious ones. Come in closer and fuller. Come into My Holy Place, My place of intercession, My place of high praises. Come to My Pentecost. Let Me immerse you in My precious Holy Spirit and endow you with gifts and with the power of My lordship that you may be to the praise of My glory, My presence, that the world may know you and see you and, in knowing you and seeing you, they will come to know Me and see Me. They will see that you have been with Me. They will see that you are with Me and that I am with you. I am the Presence in the midst of you. Come! Let me immerse you in My Spirit.

Come even closer, My holy ones, My precious ones. Come into the Holy of Holies, the Most Holy Place—to that place in the spirit where I am the only thing that matters, where you have a full revelation of who I am in you, through you, and among you.

Come to My feast of Tabernacles, dwell with Me in the fullness of My Spirit.

Let me take you by the hand and lead you to the Outer Court of Passover, onward to the Holy Place of Pentecost, ultimately into the intimacy of the Most Holy Place of Tabernacles.

Let Me be your glory. Let Me fill you with My glory. Those of you who are content to stay in the Outer Court have My life, My Spirit, My grace, and My mercy, but only in thirtyfold measure of My fullness. I desire more for you.

Those of you who come to the Pentecost of the Holy Place and choose to camp out there and not move on with Me have My Spirit. You have many riches, you have revelation, and you have knowledge, but you can only have a sixtyfold measure of My fullness. I desire more for you.

Those of you who choose to stay in the Outer Court of Passover or the Holy Place of Pentecost and are not hungering and thirsting to press on into the Most Holy Place of Tabernacles will find that your oil will be shy at the sound of My trump. You will find that the cares of this world will easily carry you back to Egypt where you came from. That is not My desire for you.

I desire fullness of joy in your presence. I desire that you come fully into My presence that you may enjoy the fullness of My presence, My joy, My love, My mercy, and My kindness toward you.

There is always another step you can take, a deeper walk with Me. It is yours. I am yours. I am yours a hundredfold if you pant after Me, long for Me, desire Me even as the hart pants for the water brooks *(Ps.42:1)*.

Do you hear the trumpet sounding in your heart, calling deep unto deep?

"But Lord," you say, "I am afraid. I have never passed this way before."

I say to you, fix your eyes upon Me. Look and see that My hand is extended to you as it was to Peter who—out of his exuberance to come to Me, to be with Me, to allow Me to be the Presence in his midst—leaped out of the ship and began to walk on water toward Me *(Matt. 14:25-32)*.

Yes. The water was deep, but I was with him. I carried him through. Even when he began to sink in a moment of fear, doubt, and unbelief, I lifted him up. I carried him through, not on the basis of his faith, but upon Mine.

So it is with you, My beloved. Take My hand and let Me take you from glory to glory, faith to faith, deep unto deep, unto fullness in Me.

the comission

t w e n t y - s i x

Alll authority has been given to Me in heaven and in earth. "Go, therefore, and teach all nations, baptizing them in the name of the Father, and of the Son, and of the Holy Ghost; teaching them to observe all things whatsoever I have commanded you. And, lo, I am with you always, even unto the end of the world. Amen" *(Matt. 28:18-20)*.

Take this promise, this assurance of My presence with you wherever you go, day or night, week in or week out, year after year, for "I am with you even unto the completion of the age."

I am the Presence in the midst of you.

"Now unto Him who is able to keep you from falling and to present you faultless before the presence of His glory with exceeding joy, to the only wise God our Savior, be glory and majesty, dominion and power, both now and forever. Amen."
(Jude 24-25)

In Search of Dad: Calling Forth the Dad within the Man

God led the author to search for information about his dad, but it soon became clear that he was looking for more than that; He was looking for *the dad* within himself.

The dad is a supernatural, transcending power that flows from Father-God enabling men to be godly fathers to their families.

God is calling forth *the dad* within men today that He might restore family as He intended, bestow the blessing upon family as He desires, and ultimately have a spiritual family for Himself in all eternity.

In Search of Dad is a prophetic book intended to call forth *the dad* power within men today. The book is in keeping with the spirit of Malachi 4:6, "…and He shall turn the heart of the fathers to the children, and the heart of the children to the fathers." It is especially useful as a study book with men's meetings.

Book specifications: Paper back, 192 pages, 5 1/2″ x 8 1/2″
ISBN 0-9647766-1-8

Ingathering Press
306 Cumberland Cove Rd.
Monterey, TN 38574
931-839-8078

ORDER FROM
Ingathering Press, 4809 Honey Grove Dr., Antioch, TN 37013
phone 615-333-6958   fax 615-834-6194

The Crucified Ones: Calling Forth the End-Time Remnant

God is going to have a people who walk in radical obedience to Him, a people who are no longer content with having to go back to the cross time and time again for forgiveness of sins but are willing to be taken through the cross to be baptized into Jesus' death and raised to resurrection life.

The book, *The Crucified Ones: Calling Forth the End-Time Remnant*, is for such a people as this. It points to the people of God who have gone from the Outer Court of Passover, through the Holy Place of Pentecost, to enter the Most Holy Place of Tabernacles.

This book will confirm what many of you already sense, that there is more. It will call forth that more as you become more willing to "present your bodies a living sacrifice, holy, acceptable unto God, which is your reasonable service" (Romans 12:1). The scripture says that "they loved not their lives unto the death" (Revelation 12:11).

Read about the crucified ones and allow the Holy Spirit to press you "toward the mark for the prize of the high calling of God in Christ Jesus" (Philippians 3:14).

Book specifications: Paper back, 121 pages, 5 1/2″ x 8 1/2″
ISBN 0-9647766-0-X